SHOULD YOU BELIEVE

# WIKIPEDIA?

Online Communities and the
Construction of Knowledge

AMY S. BRUCKMAN

CAMBRIDGE
UNIVERSITY PRESS

# CAMBRIDGE
## UNIVERSITY PRESS

University Printing House, Cambridge CB2 8BS, United Kingdom

One Liberty Plaza, 20th Floor, New York, NY 10006, USA

477 Williamstown Road, Port Melbourne, VIC 3207, Australia

314–321, 3rd Floor, Plot 3, Splendor Forum, Jasola District Centre,
New Delhi – 110025, India

103 Penang Road, #05-06/07, Visioncrest Commercial, Singapore 238467

Cambridge University Press is part of the University of Cambridge.

It furthers the University's mission by disseminating knowledge in the pursuit of education,
learning, and research at the highest international levels of excellence.

www.cambridge.org
Information on this title: www.cambridge.org/9781108490320
DOI: 10.1017/9781108780704

© Amy S. Bruckman 2022

This publication is in copyright. Subject to statutory exception and
to the provisions of relevant collective licensing agreements,
no reproduction of any part may take place without the written
permission of Cambridge University Press.

First published 2022

Printed in the United Kingdom by TJ Books Limited, Padstow Cornwall

*A catalogue record for this publication is available from the British Library.*

*Library of Congress Cataloging-in-Publication Data*
NAMES: Bruckman, Amy, author.
TITLE: Should you believe Wikipedia? : online communities and the construction of
   knowledge / Amy S. Bruckman, Georgia Institute of Technology.
DESCRIPTION: Cambridge, United Kingdom ; New York, NY : Cambridge University Press,
   2022. | Includes bibliographical references and index.
IDENTIFIERS: LCCN 2021031711 (print) | LCCN 2021031712 (ebook) | ISBN 9781108490320
   (hardback) | ISBN 9781108748407 (paperback) | ISBN 9781108780704 (epub)
SUBJECTS: LCSH: Online social networks. | Internet–Social aspects. | Internet–Psychological
   aspects. | Internet users–Psychology. | Knowledge, Theory of
CLASSIFICATION: LCC HM742 .B78 2022 (print) | LCC HM742 (ebook) | DDC 302.23/1–dc23
LC record available at https://lccn.loc.gov/2021031711
LC ebook record available at https://lccn.loc.gov/2021031712

ISBN 978-1-108-49032-0 Hardback
ISBN 978-1-108-74840-7 Paperback

Cambridge University Press has no responsibility for the persistence or accuracy
of URLs for external or third-party internet websites referred to in this publication
and does not guarantee that any content on such websites is, or will remain,
accurate or appropriate.

For Pete, Noah, and Evan

# SHOULD YOU BELIEVE WIKIPEDIA?

As we interact online we are creating new kinds of knowledge and community. How are these communities formed? How do we know whether to trust them as sources of information? In other words, should we believe Wikipedia? This book explores what community is, what knowledge is, how the internet facilitates new kinds of community, and how knowledge is shaped through online collaboration and conversation. Along the way the author tackles issues such as how we represent ourselves online and how this shapes how we interact, why there is so much bad behavior online, and what we can do about it. And the most important question of all: What can we as internet users and designers do to help the internet to bring out the best in us all?

AMY S. BRUCKMAN is Regents' Professor and Senior Associate Chair in the School of Interactive Computing at the Georgia Institute of Technology, where she studies online communities. Bruckman received her PhD from the MIT Media Lab in 1997. She is a Fellow of the ACM and a member of the SIGCHI Academy. She founded her first online community in 1993, and has been teaching the class "Design of Online Communities" at Georgia Tech since 1998. She currently helps moderate a number of large online communities.

# CONTENTS

## ACKNOWLEDGMENTS

I had so much fun writing this book – I'm actually sad that it's done. First and foremost, I'd like to thank my husband Pete Weimann and my sons Noah and Evan Weimann, who listened to me ramble about the book over dinner and on long hikes for years. Evan, thanks for figuring out where to stick the privacy content that needed a place, and I'm sorry there are two anecdotes about your brother and none about you.

I'd like to thank my mother, Cynthia Zucker, for the *World Book Encyclopedia,* and my stepfather, Bernie Zucker, for teaching me about free speech starting at age nine. You are the best parents a person could hope for. I wish my father Robert Bruckman was here to see the finished book – he would be proud.

I found starting this project intimidating. Sherry Turkle gave me excellent advice on the book proposal process, and also told me that my draft chapter was actually good. Coming from Sherry, that meant a lot. I took one class from Sherry in grad school and worked as her research assistant for half a summer, but how I see people's relationship to computing was profoundly shaped by what I learned from her.

I'd like to thank Nancy Baym for her words of wisdom on why writing a book can be an emotional roller coaster. That helped me throughout this process. Warm thanks to everyone who gave helpful comments on the book proposal, including Gilda Bruckman, Joseph Calamia, Scott Counts, Eric Gilbert, Mark Guzdial, and Barry Wellman.

I'd like to thank the people I asked about climate change for the intro to Chapter 3: Eshwar Chandrasekharan, Michaelanne Dye, J. Alex Godwin, Beki Grinter, Jochen Rick, and Eva Sharma.

Andrea Wiggins Grover helped me with the section on citizen science. Keith Hampton gave invaluable comments on the chapter on community. I couldn't have written Chapter 8 without the brilliant comments I received from David Karger. Wikipedia regular WereSpielChequers gave helpful comments on the Wikipedia chapter.

It was a great pleasure to locate my undergraduate professor for history of physics, Gerald Holton, and tell him that I still remember his class fondly. Thank you Professor Holton for your comments on the philosophy of science content in Chapter 3.

I'm grateful to all the students who gave comments on draft chapters assigned in class, especially Beatriz Palacios Abad, Suood Alroomi, D. Scott Appling, Stephanie Baione, Jennifer Guzdial, Hannah Tam, and Jordan Taylor. Thanks also to former student Vanessa Rood Weatherly and Sijia Xiao. Big thanks to PhD student Daniel Nkemelu for letting me put your homework in the book.

I am not trained as an epistemologist. I am grateful to the real epistemologists on the Facebook group Social Epistemology Network who provided helpful references. I would be lost without your help.

My Reddit moderator friends have tolerated my rambling about this book project almost as much as my family. Thanks especially to Elizabeth Crocker, Adrian de Novato, Joshua Landman, Benjamin Lippi, Claudia Lutz, Thorbjörn Sievert, and Colin Sullender.

Thanks to Georgia Tech for being a great place to work. Ayanna Howard's time as chair of the School of Interactive Computing matched the time I was writing this book almost exactly, start to finish. I am grateful for all her support – I can't imagine a more supportive boss. My colleague Colin Potts has encouraged me throughout this process, and is my role model for computer scientists who spend too much time reading philosophy.

I have worked with so many wonderful students at Georgia Tech. Everything in this book has evolved through conversations with my graduate students and students in my classes. Thanks especially to my current and former PhD students Julia Deeb-Swihart, Jill Dimond, Betsy DiSalvo, Michaelanne Dye, Jason Elliott, Jason Ellis, Casey Fiesler, Andrea Forte, Sucheta Ghoshal, Shagun Jhaver, Camille Harris, Jim Hudson, Kurt Luther, Sarita Schoenebeck, and José Zagal, and to my advisors when I was a graduate student, Glorianna Davenport and Mitchel Resnick.

I was fortunate to work with Lauren Cowles at Cambridge University Press. Her hard work and ninja editing skills made this a much better book, and I am grateful.

INTRODUCTION  Design and
           Social Behavior

I n 2004, my son Noah was turning one year old and
  I had a problem: How do I make him a birthday cake?
He was seriously allergic to dairy, soy, and egg. A mis-
read food label or a bite snuck from another child's plate
at daycare could send us to the emergency room. But he
was turning one – I wanted him to have birthday cake.
I found a website called kidswithfoodallergies.org, and
asked on the forum there: Did anyone have a dairy-,
soy- and egg-free cake recipe? In response to my query,
I got a flurry of warm welcomes from parents on the site.
They shared an excellent safe cake recipe, and provided a
host of other support. Parents on the site helped me figure
out how to make a clear and effective allergy-awareness
sheet for his daycare teachers. They shared tips for how to
safely order food in a restaurant. Their experience was
invaluable, and they also were emotionally supportive in a
way no one else could be. Parenting an allergic toddler is
stressful, and they understood completely.

    After a few months on the site, I started welcoming
new members and answering their questions. I became a
local expert on a few topics. Together, the community of
parents *built up a body of shared knowledge*. Online communities are good at constructing knowledge. As we'll see in
Chapter 3, the more you learn about the social nature of
knowledge, the more you can see why social media is good at

helping create it. Noah was lucky enough to outgrow his food allergies by the time he turned five. When I posted a picture of him eating his first piece of real pizza, other parents said it brought tears to their eyes.

This book is about the design of online communities, with an emphasis on how online communities can build (or fail to build) knowledge. To truly understand how the internet is creating knowledge, we need to understand other critical aspects of designing online groups – community, collaboration, identity, management of bad behavior, and the influence of market forces.

Online communities take many forms. I am part of a Facebook group of friends I've known since graduate school who like video games, and a subreddit of people (who I've never met) who are fans of my favorite television show. I'm part of groups for academic parents, people who volunteer to moderate a subreddit, and alumni of my elementary school, high school, college, and graduate school. I find each of these groups to be supportive in different ways.

In each group, I share different details about who I am, and I behave differently. Amy the professor, Amy the mom, and Amy the *Grey's Anatomy* fan are quite different. Norms of self-presentation are formed by a combination of software affordances and learned behavior, and those norms change group dynamics.

Each of these groups also shapes my understanding of the world. My knowledge and beliefs about how to approach safety for kids with food allergies were shaped by conversations on the food allergy group, and my opinion of the writing in *Grey's Anatomy* season seventeen has been shaped through conversation with my fellow fans. Online conversation constructs new understandings.

The internet creates new ways for us to interact, understand the world, and share our understanding with others. These processes are supported and shaped by systems that are designed by humans. This book is about the interaction between design and social behavior – all the ways that the design of the internet shapes the human behavior and knowledge that emerge as a result.

One of the most powerful affordances of the internet is its ability to create community. Before the industrial revolution in the nineteenth century, "community" was a geographically bounded concept (Hampton and Wellman 2018). Travel was slow and hence rare, and people looked to others nearby for social support and fellowship. These patterns evolved significantly with the introduction of the automobile. With the introduction of internet communication, it's possible to find community based on shared interests and values, independent of geography. The parents on the food allergy group are located all over the world, but the internet brought us together.

What is a "community"? Is a group of people interacting on a Facebook group or subreddit a "community"? In Chapter 1, I'll use ideas from the prototype theory of categories to define what a "community" is. Eleanor Rosch showed that categories in the mind are based on "prototypes" or "best examples" – a robin is a better example of a bird than an emu or a penguin. Similarly, we understand the idea of "community" in relation to prototypical communities in our minds, like small towns or church groups.

Ray Oldenburg's work on "third places" shows us why we need places that are neither work nor home, and how these supportive communities are designed. I'll show how the detailed design features of online spaces can help them serve as third places. Finally, sociological research sheds light on how online communication has reshaped the kinds of community and strong and weak ties we all rely on in our lives.

A second core contribution of the internet is its support for collaboration. In Chapter 2, I'll introduce some powerful examples of constructive uses of online collaboration – like Wikipedia and citizen science. Why do people spend hundreds of volunteer hours writing encyclopedia articles or counting birds? I'll explain the incentive structure in peer production, and what kinds of things are possible using peer production methods. I'll explore citizen science in some detail, and then introduce Yochai Benkler's theory of why peer production is important, and what factors are important for a peer production project to succeed.

Yes, people can create things together online – but are they any good? In Chapter 3, I'll answer the question of whether you should believe Wikipedia. Building on ideas from epistemology, metaphysics, and social construction of knowledge, I'll explore what it means to "know" something, and how good a job Wikipedia does at building knowledge. I will argue that "truth" exists (even if we only have indirect and unsure access to it) and knowledge is socially constructed. Social consensus is our best metric for what "is true," but sometimes that consensus can be wrong.

Chapter 4 is about "knowledge-building communities," and how the internet *changes how we think*. People increasingly come to learn things not alone but as part of a group – what everyone else around you believes shapes what you believe. The internet is a catalyst for this process. When a group of people work together to accomplish a task, they form what is called a "community of practice." Collaboratively constructing knowledge online is a process that takes place in a community of practice. I'll explain how communities of practice operate through the work of Jean Lave and Etienne Wenger. The knowledge-building process is strongly supported by elements of the software environment as well as the people working together. This is a kind of "distributed cognition," and work by Edwin Hutchins can help us understand it better.

Chapter 5 is about identity. As people interact in online venues, they need to represent who they are to others. The details of how we do this matter. Sociologist Erving Goffman explains how, in the face-to-face world, we are always performing roles. These elements of identity translate into the online world. One of the key questions for online activity is the role of anonymity. I'll explain the advantages and disadvantages of anonymous interaction. In fact, we're all really some degree of "pseudonymous" (between anonymous and identified) most of the time anyway. How identity is represented turns out to be one of the most powerful design decisions that you make in creating an online communications environment.

As most internet users are increasingly aware, interacting online is not all cute kittens and heartwarming stories. The internet can be *nasty*. In Chapter 6, I'll explore the ways we can regulate online behavior. Larry Lessig divides regulation into laws, social norms, markets, and technology.

As we'll see, ideas about "free speech" vary around the world, and laws about hate speech are quite different in the United States compared to other nations. Where we draw the line between free speech and illegal speech is the most hotly contested issue about the internet. What is at stake is not just what we all read or watch, but *who we are*. At its worst, the internet can make insane and hateful ideas seem normal, and make it easy for new people to be radicalized. On the other hand, if some speech is not allowed, who decides where to draw the line? How do we make balanced decisions about what content to allow?

How online platforms are financially supported shapes them in fundamental ways. In Chapter 7, I address how market issues shape what online sites exist and what they become. This is particularly relevant for how sites manage inappropriate content and bad behavior. What kind of behavior management takes place depends on what a site can afford. I argue that today's commercial sites can't deliver what is healthy for people or for society, because making key decisions steered by the profit motive doesn't magically make the right thing happen. We need more public investment in non-profit platforms driven by values.

Finally, in Chapter 8, I explore what we can do to make the internet better. I revisit the previous topics (community, collaboration, knowledge building, identity, behavior management, and market forces) and explore what constructive steps are possible for members of online sites, and for designers of those sites. Education is another important missing ingredient. To understand the internet, people need a more nuanced understanding of the nature of knowledge, free speech, and more.

This book is based on what I have learned iteratively over the course of more than twenty years teaching the class "Design of Online Communities" to undergraduate and graduate students at Georgia Tech. In addition to explaining online interaction, I hope you'll find the theories I introduce useful, and pick the most relevant and go read the originals.

# 1    Are Online "Communities" Really Communities?

In 2009, then-Georgia Tech master's student Vanessa Rood Weatherly and I interviewed members of the "brand community" website for owners of Mini Cooper cars. This quote from one of our research subjects has always stuck with me:

> I had a grandson who was born premature and died and everybody was just really supportive and everybody was there for me. I couldn't talk to anybody else about it on a daily basis. But I could talk [on the Mini Cooper website]. So I'd check in every day ... They were actually the first people I told when the doctor said he wasn't going to make it. That's the first place I went. I couldn't wake anybody else up at 3 in the morning. When it's like that, intense and close, it's easier to reach out to other people sometimes through the website and say it ... They weren't so close that they were that involved, so they could listen and give me advice better ... My daughter got a kick out of the fact that when she was sent to the hospital in Denver, I think she got 12 packages, cards, or flowers from people from the Mini site before she got anything from friends or family. They responded so fast. Overwhelmed by them before she ever even got anything from people who actually knew her. So like I said, it's a lot of support. (Rood and Bruckman 2009)

If it is 3 a.m. and you are facing devastating news, who would you turn to for support? It seems counterintuitive

8

that this bereaved grandmother would turn to a website for fans of a car brand. But for her, the site was a supportive community. The site was not a substitute for friends and family she knows face-to-face, but a powerful supplement.

Humans do better when we support one another – when we form supportive communities. The discipline of sociology is focused on studying all the ways that groups of people can be organized, and how that shapes the mutual support that emerges as a result. Internet communication reshapes social support in complicated ways. In this chapter, I will explain the ways that the internet has changed the forms that community takes. But first, we need to step back and define "community."

## What Is a "Community"?

What is your idealized notion of a "community"? Are the subscribers of a subreddit a community? What about people who follow a hashtag on Instagram? What really is a "community"?

Cognitive science can help answer the question. I will argue that the word "community" refers to a *category* of associations of groups of people. To understand "community," it helps to have a more nuanced view of a "category." Eleanor Rosch found that categories in the mind are not organized by simple rules of inclusion and exclusion, but by *prototypes*. Each category has one or more best or "focal" members. For example, a robin or sparrow is a better example of a bird than an ostrich or penguin (Rosch 1999). These best members are the prototypes for the category, and we understand other members in relation to the best members.

Within a category, each item has a degree of membership. The degree of membership of an item in a category depends on its similarities to and differences from the focal members (Lakoff 1987). Rosch notes, however, that talking about "the focal members" of a category is a linguistic convenience. It would be better instead to refer to the "degree of prototypicality" of each member of the category. Some that have a high degree of prototypicality we may informally call the prototypes for the category.

Surprisingly, degree of prototypicality is objective – it can be measured with reaction-time studies. A person asked if a robin is a bird will respond more quickly than when asked if a penguin is a bird. The difference is a fraction of a second, but is measurable and repeatable. These results are generally consistent across individuals from a particular cultural background (Rosch 1999).

Categories can have either clear or fuzzy boundaries. For example, the categories "car" and "truck" have fuzzy boundaries, and sport-utility vehicles (SUVs) are members of both groups. However, SUVs are somewhat remote members of both the "car" and "truck" categories – a Ford Explorer is not an ideal example of either a car or a truck.

The prototype theory of categories answers lots of hard questions. Suppose you are in an art museum looking at a monochrome, painted canvas, and wondering whether this is "art." The answer is: "Art" is a prototype-based category. Works of art with a high prototypicality for Western culture are things like the Mona Lisa by Leonardo da Vinci and paintings of water lilies by Claude Monet. A monochrome canvas "is art" in the same sense that a

Ford Explorer is a car – it's a member of the category with significant differences from the most prototypical members.

Returning to the category "community," in this light, asking whether something "is a community" is a poorly formed question unlikely to yield deep insights. The category "community" has fuzzy boundaries. Instead, we can ask how similar a particular group is to our ideal models of community. This is a more productive line of inquiry, because it challenges us to reflect on the nature of our prototypical models of community, and explore in detail their specific features and why each feature might or might not matter (Bruckman 2006).

The notion of "community" is culturally relative. For many Americans, our prototypical communities are small towns and religious congregations. These are groups of people who see one another regularly and have shared interests. Everyone understands the idea of community in relation to different prototypes, and people from other cultures have different ideal models.

Different sorts of community provide diverse kinds of value to their members. One value that our prototypical congregation or small town might provide is support in times of crisis. By that metric, the Mini Cooper online community was successful. The group provided the bereaved grandmother with someone to talk with (at any hour of night), and condolence cards and flowers that arrived before those from other friends. Howard Rheingold's beautiful chapter "The Heart of the WELL" in his book *The Virtual Community* documents a host of ways that members of The WELL (an early and influential bulletin board system) supported one another – like rallying around the parent of a child with leukemia, and researching how to arrange a medical evacuation for a member who became seriously ill in New Delhi (Rheingold 1993). Help in times of crisis is just one element of social support that is easy to identify. Nancy Baym writes that it is common "to find members of online communities and social networks providing one another with the sort of emotional support often found in close relationships" (Baym 2010).

Thinking about "community" and how it manifests online, key questions to ask are:

- What features of face-to-face communities provide meaningful support?
- How can we design online sites to provide those kinds of value to their members?
- In what ways can online interaction provide new forms of support that are not possible face-to-face?

For completeness, we must also ask:

- In what ways can face-to-face communities sometimes be oppressive, and how can we lessen the downsides when groups interact online?

## Social Capital

In a famous paper, sociologist Robert Putnam collected data on how many Americans join civic associations, and found that the proportion of people who participate in such associations dropped dramatically from the 1960s to the 1990s.

As one example of declining civic connection, he found that people were still bowling, but joining fewer bowling leagues. His paper and subsequent book were called "Bowling Alone," and became influential in part because of the catchy title. He speculates on a variety of reasons for these trends. For example, during this period the number of women who work outside the home rose. Many stay-at-home mothers contribute much of the labor for civic organizations, and working women have less time to volunteer. Second, he speculates that time spent watching television (which was high during those years) might discourage in-person activity (Putnam 1995).

Are we all bowling alone? Does it matter? These are important questions for sociology, the study of society. One way sociologists measure social support is with the concept of "social capital." Social capital is defined as "the sum of the resources embedded in social structure, or the potential to access resources in social networks for some purposeful action" (Appel et al. 2014). Ties that we make in one context may later be useful in others, providing information, influence, and solidarity (Sandefur and Laumann 1998; cited in Adler and Kwon 2002). Participation in civic organizations is one way that we can build social capital, getting to know others in our local communities. If participation in such organizations has declined, can the internet help increase our connectedness in new ways (Resnick 2001; Wellman et al. 2001)?

## Strong and Weak Ties

An important aspect of the impact of the internet on social capital is the distinction between "strong" and "weak" ties, first articulated by Mark Granovetter in his landmark paper "The Strength of Weak Ties" (Granovetter 1973). A strong tie is a close friend or family member – someone you would ask to loan you money or to take you to the doctor. A weak tie is an acquaintance – like a childhood friend you haven't seen in a few years, someone you used to work with, or a friend-of-a-friend who you've met a few times. A weak tie is someone you could ask a question.

Weak ties have surprising power. When Granovetter surveyed people about how they got their current job, most people learned about the opportunity through a weak tie. This makes sense because your strong ties connect you to a relatively small number of people, and your weak ties can connect you to orders of magnitude more.

Connections among strong ties create *bonding capital*. Weak ties provide *bridging capital*. You are likely a member of a number of highly interconnected groups – like your family and the people at your workplace or school. Those people all know one another. Within a circle of tightly connected individuals, strong ties provide access to a bounded number of people and ideas. Now let's suppose I have a weak tie to someone at another university. That person can introduce me to many people at their university, creating a bridge between otherwise separate social networks. Knowing someone who is part of a different social group is a bridge to a large number of new ties, one degree of separation away.

Knowing people with a wide variety of life experiences and knowledge is useful because they can assist you in different situations. If you are suddenly diagnosed with an illness, you might use a large social network to find someone else who has that illness and can tell you about it. If you are moving to a different city, having a large social network means you might be able to connect to someone who can tell you what neighborhoods are good to live in.

Intriguingly, having more ties gives people a broader perspective that helps them to have good ideas. Ronald Burt studied the creation of innovative ideas within a company, and found that people who have more connections across different groups are more likely to contribute good ideas (Burt 2004). If the company is facing a crisis, the person who has chatted with someone in the London office and also knows the person who manages shipping and receiving is more likely to understand the broader problem than someone who only knows people in their own work group. Weak ties – especially ones that bridge groups – are powerful.

With a bit of background on the power of weak ties, it's easy to see the value of internet communication in enhancing social capital. Computer-mediated communication is spectacular at maintaining weak ties. We use platforms like Facebook to keep in touch with old friends from school and past workplaces. Social media connects us to friends of friends, which massively expands our social networks. And it's easy to meet new people online who can become new weak ties. Online social networks enhance bridging capital (Ellison et al. 2007). Online interaction also tends to encourage face-to-face interaction (Hampton et al. 2011). Online and face-to-face community are mutually reinforcing.

## Persistent and Pervasive Community

Social capital mediated by networks is different from face-to-face social capital in interesting ways. Keith Hampton notes that the new social capital is more *persistent* and *pervasive* (Hampton 2016).

Mobility is one cause of reduced connectedness. Social networks facilitate persistent ties and are "a counter-force to mobility" (Hampton and Wellman 2018). It's increasingly easy to stay in touch with people you haven't seen face-to-face for many years. Staying in touch requires effort, but it helps that many networks enable person-to-network communications – one message can be seen by many people. Contrast the effort needed to painstakingly write individual holiday cards to a long list of people versus the effort of posting a holiday message on a social network. Personalized messages are more powerful, but the social network message still has value and requires a tiny fraction of the effort. When I posted on Facebook that I had signed the contract to write this book, 155 people "reacted" to the post, and thirty-two left a congratulatory comment. Commenters include: family, faculty and staff at my university, faculty at other universities, former students, graduate-school classmates, two fellow moderators from Reddit, and a close friend of my mother. I was able to reach all those people by just typing a few lines of text.

Hampton writes that pervasive awareness "is an affordance of the ambient nature of digital communication technologies that provides knowledge of the interests, location, opinions, and activities embedded in the everyday life events of one's social ties" (Hampton 2016). Being generally aware of what's going on with members of my social network makes that network more potentially useful to me – through social media, I know who recently vacationed at the spot I am considering going to, who lives in the town I'm visiting, and whose teenager recently, like mine, learned to drive. This general awareness enhances the social capital I find in my weak ties.

Co-located community can have serious downsides. Hampton and Wellman write that "The nature of community in the nineteenth century, or in nearly any form where people lived in a densely knit network of close ties, had its drawbacks: the density of relations implied a high degree of conformity to similar beliefs, backgrounds, and activities. Rigid hierarchies governed who could communicate with whom" (Hampton and Wellman 2018, 644). Individuality and freedom don't always thrive when your business is everyone's business. Escaping the intolerance of old-style communities is a plus. Unfortunately, some of that intolerance is being recreated by computer networks. Hampton and Wellman note that this is increasingly apparent in trends toward online public shaming and doxing (revealing personal information of otherwise anonymous or pseudonymous individuals). I'll talk more about these downsides in Chapter 6.

Some side-effects of the new persistent and pervasive form of community are surprising. One is the *cost of caring*. Through social networks, we can become aware of tragedies that befall weak ties. Without social networks, I might not know about the tragic death of my college roommate's cousin. Knowing about it, though, causes me genuine stress (Hampton et al. 2015).

Another surprising side-effect is the *spiral of silence*. If you feel your listeners are unlikely to agree with you, you are less likely to speak up about an issue. The communications literature has long documented this phenomenon in face-to-face settings. Remarkably, Hampton found that people who interact more online are less likely to speak up about an issue both online and in person. Online interaction heightens your awareness that others might find your views disagreeable, and this lowers your likelihood to discuss controversial issues both online and in person (Hampton et al. 2014). Although we have an idealized notion that online discussion can enhance the public sphere, with citizens engaging with the important issues of the day, this can't happen in reality if no one is willing to discuss difficult topics and there are no spaces that foster civil discussion of difficult issues.

## Third Places

Some online spaces are more successful than others in helping members to develop or maintain social ties. What are the design features that help? One first step to answering that question is to better understand what features of physical spaces are conducive to more beneficial social contact.

In 1989, sociologist Ray Oldenburg published a book with the wonderful title, *The Great Good Place: Cafés, Coffee Shops, Community Centers, Beauty Parlors, General Stores, Bars, Hangouts, and How They Get You Through the Day*

(Oldenburg 1989). Oldenburg is a qualitative researcher. Quantitative researchers like Robert Putnam count things – such as the number of people who join parent–teacher associations (PTAs) or bowling leagues. Qualitative sociology is closer to anthropology. Oldenburg spent a whole lot of time in bars and cafés and observed interactions there. His basic research question is: What sort of value do these spaces provide for their members?

Oldenburg argues that we all need a "third place" – a place that is neither work nor home. Work and home don't satisfy all of a person's need for social contact. Consequently, he spent years studying informal public life in a variety of settings. His findings are instructive as we begin to think about how to design online "third places."

First, Oldenburg notes that the third place should be *neutral ground*. No one is hosting and no one is a guest – those gathered are on an equal footing. It also needs a *proximate location* and long hours, so people can come and go with ease. Oldenburg notes that "the activity that goes on in third places is largely unplanned, unscheduled, unorganized, and unstructured. Here, however, is the charm. It is just these deviations from the middle-class penchant for organization that give the third place much of its character and allure that allow it to offer a radical departure from routines of home and work" (Oldenburg 1989, 33).

Oldenburg emphasizes that the third place is a leveler. He writes that "there is a tendency for individuals to select their associates, friends, and intimates from among those closest to them in social rank. Third places, however, serve to expand possibilities ... Within third places, the charm and flavor of one's personality, irrespective of his or her station in life, is what counts" (Oldenburg 1989, 24).

The tone of the third place is cheerful, and the mood is playful. Activity is generally unplanned. The main activity is conversation. Consequently, games best suited to the third place are those that promote conversation. For example, it's easier to chat while playing darts than while playing a video game.

The regulars (the people who reliably attend) are the heart of the third place. They serve as social glue, connecting other people who may miss one another by coming at different times. They also establish the social norms of the space – people follow the lead of the regulars in understanding how to behave.

Oldenburg observes that people arriving at the third place are greeted with different degrees of enthusiasm. Most warmly greeted is the prodigal regular – the person who everyone knows but who has been absent for a while. The regular is next most welcome, followed by a regular with a guest. Next most warmly welcomed is the pair of newcomers. The lone newcomer is slowest to be welcomed into the group. This order of acceptance captures the social dynamic – who the attendees are and how they relate to one another.

Traditional third places are often single-gender. This may be an anachronism in current times. I'll talk more about single-gender online spaces in Chapter 5.

Finally, third places often have a plain appearance. The third place is where the regulars and their friends and guests hang out, and unknown strangers are not necessarily welcome. In valuing fellowship and conversation, Oldenburg prefers a third place that is more like a local pub where you stop by in casual clothes than a trendy spot where you dress to impress and hope to see celebrities. These are two different styles of spaces and both have functions for different people.

While Oldenburg studied pubs and coffee shops, William Whyte did a similar study of open-air places in cities. What makes one public square fill with people when the weather is nice, and another remain empty? Whyte studied public spaces in cities, starting with parks and public squares in New York City, and found an interesting set of design criteria. First, more successful spaces are partially enclosed but still inviting. Enclosure helps create a sense of "place." However, the location needs to be visible from surrounding spaces, so people can be enticed to enter. It helps if the space has a central focus of interest – a feature to draw people in. Further, a successful public square should have affordances for human activity – like shuffleboard or chess. Whyte also notes that a good public space needs basic amenities, such as places to sit, water to drink, and restroom facilities (Whyte 1964).

## Online Third Places

The study of places where face-to-face sociability is successful provides a wealth of insights for the design of online communities. We can, for example, see most of the features noted by Oldenburg and Whyte in the Mini Cooper car site. The *central feature of interest* – the thing that draws people in – is an interest in the Mini car brand. This also creates Whyte's *sense of enclosure* – this is not a space for anyone, but for people who have something in common (a car brand).

However, once people have arrived in this shared space, the conversation ranges well beyond cars. *Conversation is the main activity.* The space is a *leveler*, with people from a range of different backgrounds communicating on an equal footing. Activity is *unplanned.* It is *easy to access* (Oldenburg's proximate location is especially true online), and has the most accommodating hours – it is always open, and had active participants when our bereaved grandmother needed support in the middle of the night. The presence of people from multiple time zones takes Oldenburg's notion of *long hours* to a new level – even if most people in your time zone are asleep, people are awake somewhere else in the world.

Oldenburg's idealized portrait of a pub and Whyte's portrait of a city park or square are highly proto-typical members of the category of "third place." As we design online spaces (like brand communities, subreddits, Facebook groups, or multi-user virtual-reality spaces), we can draw design inspiration from our knowledge of these examples.

The clearest analog between face-to-face third places and virtual ones is the role of the regulars. In an online site, some people are always there and know everyone. They form a kind of social glue between members. They can introduce you to someone else you may not have met, and catch you up on what happened while you were away. This is as strong a phenomenon on a small Facebook group or subreddit as it is in a pub.

Furthermore, the regulars set the tone for how one behaves in a space. Since they are often there and are known by everyone, others take their cues on how to behave from the regulars. People are expected to behave differently in a tea shop versus a biker bar. The way people learn how to behave in each kind of space is through observation of others in the space, especially the regulars. Online, you also behave differently in the fun, anything-goes Mini Cooper site compared to the more traditional, proper Campbell's Soup site (as Rood discovered in her research) (Rood and Bruckman 2009). Online, the regulars are often also moderators – people empowered to decide what content is acceptable. In that case they literally establish the social norms of a site.

The visual design of a space also provides important cues on how to behave (Bruckman 1996). The architecture (big windows and high ceilings, or low ceiling and no windows?), furnishings (white table cloths or old wooden tables?), and attire of other patrons (business attire or jeans and lots of leather?) implicitly tell people who belongs in a space and how one is supposed to behave there. The visual design of online spaces can similarly communicate expectations. Communicating with design is easier in a more visual space like a 3D virtual world than a simple website, but even the simplest design communicates something by its graphics, font, and layout. Deliberately unfancy presentation also communicates expectations (Pater et al. 2014).

Face-to-face communities come in a wide variety of types – for example, members of the PTA, the people who frequent a particular café, or the kids on a youth sports team and their coaches and parents. These represent "genres" of community. Online groups similarly have a wide variety of genres – like health support, technical support, alumni of a particular class at a school, or people interested in a particular issue. As designers of spaces that hope to promote supportive interactions among individuals, we can draw design inspiration from what we know about other groups (on- and offline).

## Social Roles

In face-to-face communities, people take on many different social roles. The same thing happens online. One early and insightful account of people taking on different roles in an online site is Richard Bartle's classic paper "Hearts, Diamonds, Clubs, Spades: Players Who Suit MUDs" (Bartle 1996). "MUD" stands for "multi-user dungeon," and MUDs were early multiplayer online games built entirely out of text. Many MUDs were a kind of Dungeons & Dragons game where you try to kill monsters and find magic treasure. Bartle observed there were four different kinds of players: achievers, explorers, socializers, and killers. Explorers like to interact with the world (finding all the unusual places); achievers like to act on the world (win the game); socializers like to interact with people; and killers like to act on other people (attacking the helpless). He presents this in a chart (Figure 1.1)

Most intriguingly, Bartle found that there is a kind of ecosystem among the different kinds, and having all four creates a social balance. For example, if the players of a MUD are all achievers, then people are obsessed with

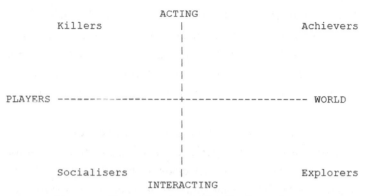

**Figure 1.1** Player types in a MUD (Bartle 1996).

gameplay and the other players become irrelevant. If the players are all socializers, then there is no gameplay, and it might as well just be a chatroom. The presence of a few killers creates challenge for the achievers and explorers, and gives the socializers something to talk about. A balance among the four types creates more satisfying patterns of interaction.

In addition to there being lots of types of users, no person's role is static – each person plays a different role in a community over time. Every "regular" was once a new-comer. Designer Amy Jo Kim documents "the membership lifecycle" in her book *Community Building on the Web* (Kim 2000). People joining a new online community start as visitors, and then may progress to novice, regular, leader, and elder. Kim presents detailed design strategies for how a site designer/manager can support members at each of these stages – how to "welcome your visitors, instruct your novices, reward your regulars, empower your leaders, and honor your elders" (Kim 2000). Just like Bartle's player types, there are dynamic social balances among these different groups. We need the right number of each kind. For example, having both too many and too few novices leads to problems, relative to the number of leaders available to help the novices.

Bartle and Kim uncovered these roles through extensive, hands-on experience with online sites. In some cases, the roles aren't self-evident. Eric Gleave and colleagues note that social roles have *behavioral regularities* and *network properties* – things you do, and patterns of who you interact with (Gleave et al. 2009). You can use both qualitative and quantitative analysis methods to uncover roles in traces of online behavior. For example, analyzing data from an online discussion site, they observed three types of participants: answer people, discussion people, and discussion catalysts. Answer people do most of the work of answering questions. Discussion people talk to many others and connect conversations. Discussion catalysts tend to start long threads of conversation. Each of these roles has different things they do and different patterns of who they talk with. Figuring out what different roles people fill in a community can help a designer make sure to support each role, and encourage people to take on roles that are needed.

One final important form of participation is *listening*. Preece and Nonnecke studied lurkers in online sites – people who listen but do not contribute. They make a compelling argument that lurking is a valid form of participation in itself (everyone can't talk all the time – someone has to listen!) (Nonnecke and Preece 2000).

Intriguingly, they found that the lurking percentage is different in discussion groups dedicated to different topics. For example, there are many more lurkers in technical support groups than in health support. In a technical support group, when a question is answered, the conversation is usually over. In a health support group, others can still chime in with personal experiences and supportive statements. As a result, the overall lurking rate is higher for technical support.

Technical support and health support are *genres* of online discussion, which tend to foster different patterns of interaction among participants. We can understand most online interaction in relation to its relevant genre, and we are still in the early stages of understanding what genres of online interaction are significant.

## Social Norms

Each type of community fosters different patterns of human interaction. People behave a particular way in a technical support group compared to a health support group, and even quite differently in one technical support group versus another. Behavior can be dramatically different even across examples of the same genre of community. For example, novice questions are warmly welcomed on the subreddit r/learnpython. If a question is not clear or has been asked before, the response is still usually helpful. Beginners are welcome. In contrast, the website StackOverflow insists that all questions be new. Repeat questions and poorly formulated questions are "closed" and receive no answer. Mistakes or ignorance are not tolerated, and novices generally find the site intimidating. The two sites are intended for different audiences, and this is communicated to people in both direct and subtle ways. What kind of behavior is encouraged and how people relate to one another are quite different across these programming support groups.

How do people in the Mini Cooper car community learn how to behave there? How did it come to pass that the rules for what is appropriate are so different in the Campbell's Soup community? "Social norms" are the unwritten rules for behavior that tend to emerge in groups. Much activity in any online group is governed by those norms. *Where do the norms come from, and how can site designers shape them?* This is the overarching, core question for much of the design of social spaces. Everything I am presenting in this book (community in this chapter, identity in Chapter 5, managing bad behavior in Chapter 6, etc.) addresses different aspects of this question.

In a study of people who share fan fiction online, Casey Fiesler found that people learn social norms, first, by observing the behavior of members of the group. The underlying values of the community shape those norms. As we saw, the regulars are key to a group. People especially observe behavior of the regular members to learn how they should behave (Fiesler and Bruckman 2019). The more a group leader is viewed as a prototypical member, the more that person can help shape group norms by behaving differently to deliberately influence others (Hogg and Reid 2006). This is why "reward your regulars" and "empower your leaders" are core maxims for online community design, in Amy Jo Kim's analysis (Kim 2000).

The topic of the nature of social norms and how to shape them is a subject of great interest in several research fields, especially social psychology and communications (Lapinski and Rimal 2005). Regarding the design of online communities, the important point to note is how those norms emerge differently in different subgroups.

Social norms are often not followed. Members of a group may misunderstand norms, or may deliberately violate them. In Chapter 6, I'll explore how we decide what online behavior is unacceptable for a given context, and what to do about it.

## Theoretical Summary

The word "community" refers to a category in the mind. In cognitive science, the theory of prototype-based categories suggests that categories are defined by best examples (Lakoff 1987; Rosch 1999). We understand members of a category in relation to members that have a high degree of typicality. For the category community, our best members might, for example, be a small town or religious congregation. When we try to understand what kind of value an online community provides for its members, we can compare design features and patterns of human association in that group to those of the most relevant face-to-face communities.

*Social capital* is a measure of how much people support one another in a society (Adler and Kwon 2002; Putnam 1995). People's social ties can be strong (close family and friends) or weak (acquaintances). Mark Granovetter found that weak ties are especially powerful in providing social capital. For example, in Granovetter's study, the majority of people who found a new job heard about the opportunity through a weak tie. Two kinds of social capital are *bonding* (among strong ties) and *bridging* (which leverages weak ties that cross social groups). Social networks are particularly good at enhancing weak ties and bridging capital (Ellison et al. 2007).

Social capital facilitated by computer networks is *persistent* and *pervasive*. It is easier to keep in touch with people we meet over the course of a lifetime, and maintain awareness of both their significant life events and day-to-day activities. This enhances our social capital, but has a side-effect of the *cost of caring* and makes us more vulnerable to the *spiral of silence* (Hampton 2016; Hampton et al. 2014, 2015).

*Third places* – places that are neither work nor home – provide valuable sources of social support. Studying features of face-to-face third places like pubs, cafés, and city parks can help designers of online sites (Oldenburg 1989; Whyte 1964).

In online communities, individuals take on different *social roles*. Members are at different points in the membership life cycle (Kim 2000), and even at the same stage may have self-selected different roles in the group. Social roles have different patterns of behavior and network properties (who they typically talk to), and can be uncovered through both qualitative and quantitative analysis of online activity (Gleave et al. 2009). People in different social roles create a kind of behavioral ecosystem within a group, and groups are more effective when there is a good balance among people in different roles.

## Practical Applications

Much online activity is simply individual or transactional. I order new socks, and they arrive a few days later. I search for a sports score, and a dozen sites compete to tell me who won and how the game went. However, sometimes people form groups online that are mutually supportive in interesting ways. Key concepts from sociology – social capital, strong and weak ties, bonding and bridging capital, third places, and social roles – can help us to understand those groups. Those concepts can help us to understand why some spaces are more successful than others, what kinds of support online communication can provide for members, and how to make them more effective. We can trace patterns of human association that emerge in online groups back to specific design features of the online communications platform. Analogies to face-to-face groups can provide a source of inspiration for creating innovative online sites.

2     What Can Online Collaboration
      Accomplish?

In 2006, we took our then two-year-old son to dinner at
Ted's Montana Grill, a restaurant that specializes in bison
burgers and has pictures of bison on the walls. Looking
around, he asked, "What sound does a bison make?" I told
him I really didn't know, but when we got home I opened up
YouTube and searched for "sound of a bison." And the first
search result was exactly that.

Could you have predicted this would be possible?
I know I couldn't have. I remember as a grad student chatting
with my advisor, Mitchel Resnick, about whether it would
ever be possible to search for an arbitrary word on the web
and get a meaningful result. We both agreed that was silly –
no way! Of course this was around 1992 – we were discussing
the first web browser, NCSA Mosaic. So maybe we can be
forgiven for being short-sighted. If being able to do a meaningful search for anything on the web is surprising, being able
to search for anything (like bison) on YouTube is even more
so. Sites like YouTube and Wikipedia have reached a critical
mass of content that make them truly useful.

The accomplishments of internet-supported, large-
scale collaboration are stunning. Should you be curious
about bison, you can hear and see them on YouTube and
read their complete history on Wikipedia, enabled by the
Apache web server, the Firefox browser, and the Linux
operating system. The internet has made new kinds of

collaboration possible, with surprising and impressive results. How does it all work?

In the last chapter, I explored the ways that people online form supportive communities. One of the critical things members of those communities do is to collaborate to create content. They may be constructing a useful resource (like all the videos on YouTube, or the content of Wikipedia), or just building a shared understanding. What factors make online collaborations succeed or fail? Working together, volunteers on sites like Wikipedia and YouTube have created resources of unprecedented value. This chapter explores what makes that possible.

## From the *World Book* to Wikipedia

In my childhood bedroom, the shelf still holds over four feet of heavy beige volumes: *The World Book Encyclopedia* for 1975, with "Year Books" containing updates for 1975 to 1994 (Figure 2.1). My mother, Cynthia Zucker, purchased this for

**Figure 2.1** The *World Book Encyclopedia* in my childhood bedroom.

me when I was in elementary school. For her as a single parent at the time trying to get by on her salary from a part-time job as a statistician, it was a major investment. But she felt that it was important to have a kid-friendly, comprehensive information source in the house. For people who grew up in the age of the internet, it's worth taking a moment to think about why this was important. Without any kind of internet access, if I wanted to look something up, I needed to physically go to the library. Having an encyclopedia at home was a huge help. I would not have believed you if you had told me that this would be the last encyclopedia my family would purchase, or that by the time my own children were in elementary school, paper copies of encyclopedias would be rare and largely unnecessary. As of 2021, you can still buy a paper *World Book*, but *Encyclopedia Britannica* has been online-only since 2010, and *Microsoft Encarta* was discontinued in 2009. Encyclopedias on specialized topics remain more common.

Paper encyclopedias are nearly obsolete because of the rise of Wikipedia, the internet-based encyclopedia that anyone can edit. To me, the biggest surprise in the history of collaborative computing is that Wikipedia *works*. The details of how it actually works are critical not only to understanding Wikipedia, but to understanding what else we might accomplish with this collaborative medium.

In early 2000, Jimmy Wales and Larry Sanger started to work on an online encyclopedia, called "Nupedia," with a relatively traditional publishing model. Since initial progress on creating articles was slow, they decided to use Ward Cunningham's "wiki" technology (Leuf and Cunningham

34

2001) to make a workspace to develop articles to later move to Nupedia. A wiki is a website with pages that anyone can edit. It has the important feature of unlimited version history – if someone makes a change you don't like, you can revert to any of the previous versions of the page. You can let people edit freely, because anything can be undone. As content rapidly grew on the wiki workspace, Wales and Sanger realized that the openly editable version could be the real version and not just a development workspace. In early 2001, they reserved the domain name "Wikipedia" and the wiki version became primary (Sanger 2005).

Their decision to allow anyone to edit Wikipedia was counterintuitive. You don't even need to log on to make an edit – anonymous edits are allowed. It works because enough people care about Wikipedia that deliberate vandalism or poorly thought-out changes are quickly removed. In 2004, Fernanda Viegas et al. found that vandalism was removed in 1.7 minutes if it involved an obscenity, and 2.8 minutes if it was a mass deletion (Viegas et al. 2004). Over time, a host of mechanisms have evolved to protect Wikipedia from vandalism. If a page is vandalized too many times or so controversial that people are repeatedly reverting one another's work ("edit warring"), editing of that page can be temporarily or permanently restricted to more trusted editors. Automated mechanisms ("bots") can detect and revert the most obvious vandalism (Geiger and Halfaker 2013). In Chapter 3 I'll talk about how reliable the content is, and what it means to have such a resource created by ordinary citizens rather than content experts.

As of January 2021, Wikipedia is available in 306 languages, and nineteen of these have over one million articles. Wikipedia is just one example of what can be accomplished by online collaboration. When volunteers work together online to accomplish something greater, this is often called "peer production," and it takes many forms. These include open-content publishing (Wikipedia), open-source software, citizen science, and online creative collaboration. Each has a different structure for how people work together.

Online collaboration raises many questions. What kinds of things can online collaboration accomplish? What motivates people to contribute? How can we tell if the product created is any good? One successful form of online collaboration is citizen science. Volunteers (working both online and in person) collect and analyze data about the natural world that is actually useful to scientists.

## Citizen Science

What can one scientist learn about the natural world? Would it help if they had thousands of volunteer assistants? With support from internet-based coordination software, sometimes it can. Working together, large groups of volunteers have built scientific databases of information about galaxies and bird populations, discovered the 3D structure of a protein, and even proved new mathematical theorems.

The practice of citizen science actually predates the invention of computers. For example, the Christmas Bird

Count began in 1900.[1] A common holiday pursuit at the time was the Christmas "side hunt," where hunters would compete to see who could shoot the most game. Concerned about the environmental impact, Frank M. Chapman at the American Museum of Natural History suggested that people could *count* birds rather than killing them. In 1900, twenty-seven birders counted ninety species. Over Christmas 2018 (year 119), 2,615 teams of birders counted 2,638 species and nearly forty-nine million birds (LeBaron 2019). Internet technology makes it easier to coordinate larger-scale efforts with more volunteers across a greater geographic area. For environmental projects, mobile computing lets data be directly recorded in the field (Silvertown 2009).

One of the best-known citizen science projects is Galaxy Zoo, created in 2008 by astronomers at Oxford University in the United Kingdom. Modern robot-operated telescopes can capture a massive number of images of far-away galaxies – orders of magnitude more than astronomers have time to analyze. Looking at a picture of a galaxy, is it spiral or elliptical, smooth or bulging (Pinkowski 2010)? It turns out that it's surprisingly hard for a computer to automatically classify images of galaxies. Some recent results using deep learning (a technique in machine learning) have had promising results (Khalifa et al. 2018). In 2008, a computer couldn't do a very good job of classifying galaxies, but a person could do it easily. Oxford graduate student Kevin Schawinski needed a large number of images classified for

[1] www.audubon.org/conservation/history-christmas-bird-count.

his PhD research, and realized he needed help (Spotts 2007). A website was built to let volunteers classify images.

The Galaxy Zoo website went online in 2008, and 150,000 volunteers entered fifty million classifications over a period of three weeks. They had to shut the project down for a while because volunteers had completely classified all the images in their original dataset. New datasets posted later were processed even faster. In 2009, the creators of Galaxy Zoo made a new website called "Zooniverse" to expand the approach to other kinds of data classification projects – like identifying animals in photos of the jungle, and fish in photos of the sea floor. The scope of the project has expanded beyond biology, taking on tasks like transcribing handwritten diaries of World War I soldiers or notes by artists in the Tate Museum collection (Atkinson 2009).

A key challenge for any citizen science project is the reliability of the information provided by volunteers. If one person says an image is a spiral galaxy, are they right? Maybe. But if a dozen people agree that it's a spiral, you can be fairly confident that it is. Galaxy Zoo first trains volunteers to recognize important features of images of galaxies, and then has each image evaluated by twenty separate people. In any crowd-sourcing project, you can calculate how many independent people need to process each piece of data. You simply start with a sample dataset for which you know the correct answers ("ground truth"). Next, you have a large number of people process it, and then calculate how many raters you need for a desired level of reliability. It may, for example, take six raters to get 80 percent accuracy, and fifteen raters to get 99 percent accuracy. If 99 percent accuracy is adequate, then you don't need a sixteenth rater. You can calculate how many raters are needed for a particular task.

Volunteers can sometimes *outperform experts*. In a study of the project Snapshot Serengeti on the Zooniverse platform, Swanson et al. found that agreement among a set of untrained volunteers led to 97.9 percent accuracy in animal identification, while individual experts were accurate 96.6 percent of the time. As they note, even an expert can make a mistake – particularly if they are reviewing a large number of photographs. Having confirmation from another person helps (Swanson et al. 2016). How to do citizen science well is a thriving field of research, and a key focus is how to improve data quality (Parrish et al. 2018).

Gathering field data about the environment (like the Christmas Bird Count) or doing data analysis (like Galaxy Zoo) are just two of the many kinds of projects that can be accomplished by citizen scientists. Andrea Wiggins Grover and Kevin Crowston classify citizen science activities into five categories: action (encouraging participation in local concerns using the scientific method), conservation (supporting natural resource management goals), investigation (collecting data from the physical environment), virtual (projects that are entirely online), and education (projects where outreach is the primary goal) (Wiggins and Crowston 2011). Citizen science projects require different levels of expertise and commitment on the part of volunteers. Someone classifying galaxies on Galaxy Zoo might invest a few minutes or hours. The Great Sunflower Project gathers data on bee populations. Volunteers agree to plant a particular variety of sunflower, and then submit data on how many bees visit the sunflowers for at least three five-minute periods (Domroese and Johnson 2017). In the NestWatch project from the Cornell Lab of Ornithology, volunteers may walk for hours each time they observe a nest box placed in a remote location (Cornell Lab of Ornithology n.d.). Volunteers for the Coastal Observation and Seabird Survey Team (COASST) take a six-hour training course, and agree to a year of monthly observations of a beach, looking for dead birds by the shore. Each observation can take a few hours – longer if there is a big "die off" event that needs recording (Haywood 2014). The degree of time commitment for the volunteer varies.

## Motivation in Citizen Science

Why do people contribute to citizen science projects? Dana Rotman and colleagues interviewed forty-four participants in citizen science projects in the United States, India, and Costa Rica to try to understand people's motivations in depth. Rotman found that people's *initial* motivations for joining include personal interest, possible value for their career, a desire to contribute to science, a desire to be a member of the scientific community, and a sense of social responsibility (Rotman et al. 2014).

Those factors draw people in; however, most people participate in citizen science for a relatively brief period of time. The most active users do a large fraction of the total work that volunteers contribute. Sauermann and Franzoni found that the top 10 percent of contributors to seven Zooniverse projects completed 80 percent of the work

(Sauermann and Franzoni 2015). As we'll see, other kinds of peer production like open-source software also follow this contribution pattern.

For the small number of volunteers who contribute longer term, what motivates them to stay? Rotman et al. found that people's long-term motivations were different from their initial ones. Longer term, people stay because they develop relationships with other volunteers and with scientists, and enjoy formal and informal recognition they've received for their contributions (Rotman et al. 2014).

Supporting user motivation is a priority for designers of citizen science programs. Programs need to both attract new users and encourage some of those users to become dedicated longer-term volunteers. Rotman studied users who had primarily intrinsic motivations to participate. You have intrinsic motivation when an activity is rewarding in itself, and extrinsic when the reward is separate. For example, reading a book is intrinsically motivated if you enjoy reading, and extrinsically motivated if you are trying to win a "most books read this summer" competition. Turning something into a game ("gamification") adds extrinsic motivations (i.e., points and winning). This approach was taken, for example, by the Foldit project. Participants in Foldit try to find 3D structures for proteins. Determining a protein's structure is so complex that even a supercomputer can't calculate a protein shape in a reasonable amount of time. The creator of Foldit, Seth Cooper, and colleagues created an interactive application that lets volunteers try a variety of strategies for finding an acceptable structure (one that minimizes energy held in the molecule). An initial structure for a protein is posted as a puzzle, and players compete to see who can create the lowest-energy version (Cooper et al. 2010). Players earn points for how good their solution is, and a leaderboard shows the best solutions so far for each protein. The features borrowed from video games like points and leaderboards encourage people to participate.

Foldit players can also form teams and work together on solutions to protein-folding problems. Comradery with your team members is another significant motivation to participate, and people take pride in their teams. Two Foldit teams helped discover the structure of a protein significant in the HIV virus. When the results were published, Cooper and colleagues wanted to list the players as co-authors. The players chose to list their team names ("Foldit Contenders Group" and "Foldit Void Crushers Group") on the paper, rather than their individual real names (Khatib et al. 2010).

The idea of gamifying projects of this nature was first pioneered by Luis Von Ahn. His first game was called *The ESP Game*, and had individuals look at an image and think what words another player might use to describe an object in the picture. Points are awarded if both players (who cannot talk to each other) pick the same word. In reality, the data was being used to label images – if both players respond with "dog," then there is likely a dog in the picture. The more pairs of people agree on "dog," the more we can be sure. Labels are useful for image search and for blind users accessing the web with screen readers. Players labeled ten million images in the first few months of the game's deployment (Von Ahn 2006; Von Ahn and

Dabbish 2004). In the Zooniverse project, people are willing to do repetitive labeling of pictures of galaxies for free because they enjoy contributing to science, and being part of real astronomy is exciting. With Von Ahn's *ESP Game*, people were willing to label less-exciting images. Game-like techniques are a useful tool in designing peer production systems.

Systems like the *ESP Game* are often referred to as "crowd sourcing." I'll use the terms "crowd sourcing" and "peer production" interchangeably. However, generally the term "crowd sourcing" is used when the volunteer is performing simpler tasks, like identifying images, and "peer production" is used when the volunteer is doing something more complex, like contributing one scene of an animated movie or helping to prove a mathematical theorem.

### Peer Production and Intellectual Challenge: The Polymath Project

Citizen science is just one form of online collaboration. People online collaborate to create all kinds of things – knowledge about the world, art, and even original mathematics. Much of the work people do in peer production systems is straightforward – like saying whether there's a dog in the picture or whether a galaxy is spiral or elliptical. But as Foldit showed, structuring peer production to let users make more challenging contributions is possible. Pushing this to the limit, could you use peer production to prove a mathematical theorem? This in fact is what happens on the Polymath Project.

The project was started by a famous mathematician, Timothy Gowers. Gowers is winner of the Fields Medal, which is like a Nobel Prize for math. He was quickly joined in the effort by another Fields Medalist, Terence Tao. Polymath's famous founders immediately attracted attention to the project and gave it credibility. A project like this wouldn't immediately take off if it was started by someone unknown. Gowers was interested in seeing how a diverse group of people could contribute to mathematical thinking in different ways, and wanted to see if having more participants would increase the chances of a lucky idea being found.

Polymath is organized on a blog, and people contribute by adding comments. Justin Cranshaw and Aniket Kittur studied early activity on the Polymath Project to understand what factors support and hinder the collaboration (Cranshaw and Kittur 2011). They did a detailed analysis of activity on Polymath 1, the site's first attempt to prove a theorem collaboratively. From February to May 2009, there were 1,555 comments written on fourteen blog posts. Comments that contributed significantly to the final proof received a number. In total, thirty-nine different people contributed numbered comments. The top ten contributors made 90 percent of the comments (following the same pattern we see in citizen science and open-source software). Contributors range in experience from Fields Medalists Gowers and Tao, to new assistant professors of math, to graduate students and high-school math teachers. Four contributors had no prior math publications, and six more had only one. Cranshaw notes in particular that some users who commented infrequently actually made a significant contribution to the final, successful proof.

Early on in the process, Tao proposed that each discussion thread should be limited to 100 comments. While this decision was made to limit complexity, it had the important side-effect of encouraging the leaders to write a summary of what had been discussed at the end of each thread of 100 comments. This design choice added modularity to the process. As we'll see in the next section, task modularity greatly helps collaborative work.

Polymath is an intriguing example of online collaboration, because the task is so demanding. In the next section, I'll introduce theoretical work about what peer production can accomplish.

## Understanding Online Collaboration as a Mode of Production

How is getting something done by peer production different from the task being done in other ways, like by paying a company or independent contractor to do it? Scholars from the discipline of management science have an interesting perspective, studying how our systems of rewards shape what happens in practice. I'll return to this topic in Chapter 7. Management science notes that how much you can get done on a project depends on how resource-intensive it is, in terms of both time and money. In his paper "Coase's Penguin, or, Linux and the Nature of the Firm," law professor Yochai Benkler makes a case that peer production is a fundamentally new phenomenon (Benkler 2002). In the

management literature, Ronald Coase explored the difference between "firms" and "markets." In a firm, you hire
employees and are then responsible for providing them with
office space, paying them a salary, and managing their time.
Firms are clusters of resources under managerial command,
and they have *organization costs*. If instead of hiring an
employee you recruit an outside individual or group to do
the task, you don't have those organization costs – but you
have *transaction costs*. You need to find the right person,
negotiate a price, and make a legal agreement about who
owns the results and what will happen if the work isn't
completed on time or to the correct specifications. Coase
divides the world into firm, market, and hybrid models, and
shows the dynamic between them. Benkler explains, "people
use markets when the gain from doing so, net transaction
costs, exceed gains from doing the same thing in a managed
firm, net organization costs" (Benkler 2002, 372).

So is peer production more like a firm or a market?
Benkler's answer is neither. He argues that peer production is
a fundamentally new paradigm, with profound implications.
Consider how people are assigned a particular task. In a firm
model, this is done by managerial control – managers need to
figure out who takes on what work, and match individuals'
skills, interests, and available time with the work that needs to
be done. In a market model, this is done by attaching prices to
tasks. Both of these models have major *inefficiencies* and *losses
of information*. For example, a firm might have too little work
for the number of employees (inefficiency), or managers
might not correctly understand each employee's capabilities
(loss of information). In a market, the whole process of setting

up transactions is imprecise. What if it takes a long time to find someone suitable for a task on the market (inefficiency), or if you choose someone who is not really qualified (loss of information)? In peer production, on the other hand, people self-select for tasks. This is arguably a better approach, because an individual is often the best person to understand their own capabilities and interests. Thinking about everyone self-selecting for what they best can and want to do, Benkler concludes that peer production will lead to overall better allocation of human creativity. Benkler's argument in favor of peer production rests on his assertion that on the whole an individual's judgment of their own capabilities is better than a manager's judgment. It's an intriguing empirical question to what extent this is true in specific contexts.

Peer production relies on decentralized information gathering to reduce uncertainties. Individuals (who know their capabilities) self-identify for tasks. This only works if people's judgments are good. Therefore, we have *peer review* of contributions to correct poor judgments.

This leaves two major challenges for peer production: *motivation* and *organization*. People in firms do something because their manager tells them to (and they are being paid to do what their manager requests). People in markets do something because they're being paid for the specific, individual task. Why do volunteers participate in peer production? Editors of Wikipedia, citizen science participants, and participants in other volunteer online collaborations are not told to do so by a manager and are not being paid. Why do they do it? Benkler argues that social–psychological rewards replace monetary rewards.

In 1990, I was trying to build a "smart" video-editing system in Macintosh Common Lisp (MCL) as part of my master's thesis at the MIT Media Lab. MCL had just moved to version 2.0, with major changes. MCL is open-source software – an important form of peer production of content that I'll discuss in detail later in this chapter. The new version wasn't quite done – lots of key files hadn't been converted to the new syntax. I needed to put a button on the screen and the code to make a button wasn't ported – so I ported it. In all honesty, I did it badly – someone else later had to fix it in a dozen ways. But I got it working, and my name is in the changelog. To this day, every once in a while I get email from an acquaintance saying they saw my name in the changelog for MCL, and I can't help feeling proud. The sense of pride I felt in getting credit for contributing to MCL is one example of the social–psychological rewards that Benkler refers to. Similarly, in Chapter 6, we'll see that volunteer online moderators invest time in helping manage an online group (like a Facebook group or a subreddit), because it gives them elevated status within the group, and they enjoy the sense of camaraderie among volunteers.

Benkler's second key challenge for peer production of content is *organization*. Part of what made my modest contribution to MCL possible is the division into small pieces of the work to be done. Having a range of different-size pieces will let people with different levels of commitment contribute. It helps if the pieces are independent of one another, so people can just select a piece and work on it, without having to coordinate with others. Finally, we need easy integration of these separate, contributed parts. In sum, a project is suitable for a peer production approach if it has *modularity, independent parts*, and *easy integration* of those parts.

## The Structure of Wikipedia

Wikipedia excels in Benkler's three criteria. The division into articles gives it high modularity. You can write or edit an article, a paragraph, or even just fix a single-word typo. The parts are independent from one another – it helps if the article on peanut allergy doesn't actively contradict the article on food allergy, but you can work on them separately. And the article on peanut allergy has no connection to the article on trash cans. (These are articles I have edited.) No integration of parts is needed – when you make a Wikipedia edit, it is already integrated. This is different, for example, than most data from citizen science, where meaning only emerges from integrating data from many sources. For example, information on how many bees visit one garden is not especially meaningful, but it becomes meaningful when organizers of the Great Sunflower Project aggregate data from thousands of locations. If aggregation is not necessary, the task is easier.

Wikipedia has more structure than is immediately obvious to the casual observer. As we have seen, the ability to easily undo any change is critical to allowing anyone to edit Wikipedia. Each article has a "history" tab where you can see all the past versions and compare any two versions. In addition, each article has a "talk" page where editors can discuss the article.

Wikipedia has evolved a set of policies over time that are central to keeping the site functional. One policy requires that articles take a "neutral point of view" (NPOV).[2] An encyclopedia is supposed to present an unbiased view, with all the content supported by reliable citations. Content that expresses an opinion or takes a strong stance on an issue is removed. Another key policy concerns "biographies of living persons" (BLP).[3] To avoid possibly being accused of libel and to respect the rights of living people, BLP guides editors on how to give special consideration for articles about living individuals. There are thousands of policies that continue to evolve.

Remarkably, these policies are on Wikipedia pages which are *editable themselves*. Changes to policies generally aren't made without extensive discussion on the "talk" page for that policy. In 2010, someone added my birthday to the Wikipedia article about me. Since many privacy experts recommend not sharing your birthday online to help protect against identity theft, I posted on the talk page for BLP asking if subjects of articles could ask to have their birthdays removed. The change was discussed and quickly approved, and the BLP policy was updated to say that subjects may request their birthdays not be posted. With the new policy, editors removed my birthday not only from the page about me, but also from the history of the page.

Sometimes it helps to coordinate articles in a subject area, and this is the role of "WikiProjects." Each project

---

[2]  http://en.wikipedia.org/wiki/NPOV
[3]  https://en.wikipedia.org/wiki/Wikipedia:Biographies_of_living_persons

focuses on a particular subject area, and takes "ownership" of a set of pages. For example, there are WikiProjects about military history, medicine, dinosaurs, and opera. Active WikiProjects establish standards for articles, like specifying what information should be in the information box for a dinosaur (temporal range, classification, etc.). Projects often come up with standards for article quality for the topic, rate articles for quality by those metrics, and give volunteers suggestions for what most needs attention. For example, project Opera has a "composer of the month" and "opera of the month" which they collaborate to improve. Members of WikiProjects help improve the overall coherence of Wikipedia. To return to my earlier example, members of WikiProject Medicine have checked that the article on peanut allergy doesn't contradict the more general article on food allergy.

Wikipedia is different in every language. Students in my Design of Online Communities class in 2005 compared Wikipedia in English, Spanish, Turkish, and Hindi. They found that the smaller the Wikipedia, the more article coverage was focused on things unique to that language and region. The Spanish Wikipedia covers almost as many topics as English, but the Hindi Wikipedia was at the time entirely about Hindi topics; Turkish was in the middle.

The specific content of pages differs by language as well. Machine translation technology is currently somewhat unreliable, but even if it worked optimally it would not be strategic to simply translate articles across languages. Brent Hecht created a system called Omnipedia, which let you compare the content of a page on Wikipedia in twenty-five languages. Next to the English text, it showed a translation of the same page from the other languages, so you could compare the content. For example, the page for "conspiracy theory" in the English Wikipedia talks about things like the assassination of John F. Kennedy and whether the moon landings were faked. The Dutch Wikipedia maintains a list of conspiracies specific to the Netherlands and Belgium. The German and Hebrew Wikipedias have extensive content about anti-Semitic conspiracies. The very concept of a conspiracy is culturally relative (Bao et al. 2012).

## Open-Source Software: The Cathedral and the Bazaar

While you are reading a page on peer-produced Wikipedia, you may well be using open-source software (OSS) for your internet browser (Firefox), and the content may be sent to your computer by an open-source web server (Apache). Open-source software is a powerful form of peer production with its own structure. A growing amount of the world's software is now open source. How OSS is made is an interesting contrast to the process of creating Wikipedia or citizen science.

A piece of software is complex, and often has inter-dependent parts. How is it possible for volunteers to build it? In 1997, an early pioneer of OSS development, Eric Raymond, wrote a paper about the process of OSS development, titled "The Cathedral and the Bazaar" (Raymond 1999). The "cathedral" model represents how software has been traditionally created by firms. Firms hire managers and software engineers. Managers divide the work into pieces and assign specific tasks to individual software engineers, who report to them. Often, a separate quality assurance (QA) department will later test the software. A top-down management structure organizes activity. The "bazaar" model reflects the new open-source paradigm, with a potentially chaotic flurry of activity and many self-selected participants. Raymond's essay is credited with catalyzing the OSS movement, and was itself written in open-source fashion (with corrections based on comments from readers, and a version history).

Raymond explains that a new open-source project usually begins not with a blank slate but with a partial, working, tantalizingly unfinished initial version. The person who created the initial version then becomes the project's leader. It would be difficult to attract volunteer helpers with just an idea. Having an initial working version convinces people that the project has plausible promise. As others start using the initial project, they may add features or fix bugs. They do this initially on their own copy of the project, and then send their proposed changes to the leader, asking if it could be made part of the "official" release. The leader needs to evaluate each proposed contribution and make a decision about whether to include it as it is, request changes, or reject it. This takes significant work.

The OSS development process is not "leaderless" or "democratic" – it's typically a *benevolent dictatorship*. The person who started the project is in charge. If a small group share control, that is an *oligarchy*. The Apache web server project is one example of an oligarchy (Nakakoji et al. 2002). Returning to Benkler's criteria for successful peer production, a key challenge for OSS is integration of parts. It's not possible to simply include every piece of code someone contributes to an OSS project. On Wikipedia, contributions are immediately accepted, and if they are not helpful they can be removed later. In software, a bad contribution doesn't just reduce the quality of one small part of the system – it may break it entirely. Consequently, someone needs to carefully evaluate what code to include in the official version. That role is played by the founder of the project, or sometimes by a leadership team.

Early OSS projects were accomplished using just email and mailing lists as the primary means of communication (in the mid-1990s, when Raymond made fetchmail, the project whose creation is chronicled in his paper, the web didn't even exist). You can imagine how high the email load of the leader was. Websites designed explicitly to support OSS development, such as SourceForge (founded in 1999) or GitHub (2007), make OSS development much easier, with features like version control, bug tracking, and separate discussion spaces for different issues.

Most OSS projects fail. To be successful, Raymond argues that you need both a good project and a good leader. The project needs plausible promise, and a good initial version. And it needs to be something that others need – most people contribute to OSS because they need the tool themselves (Crowston et al. 2012).

The leader of an OSS project needs enough technical skill to command respect, and the ability to recognize good ideas. Having strong interpersonal skills is also critical. Raymond writes,

> In order to build a development community, you need to attract people, interest them in what you're doing, and keep them happy about the amount of work they're doing. Technical sizzle will go a long way towards accomplishing this, but it's far from the whole story. The personality you project matters, too. It is not a coincidence that Linus [Torvalds, the leader of the Linux project] is a nice guy who makes people like him and want to help him. It's not a coincidence that I'm an energetic extrovert who enjoys working a crowd and has some of the delivery and instincts of a stand-up comic. To make the bazaar model work, it helps enormously if you have at least a little skill at charming people.

Developers of OSS projects are largely volunteers. Some corporations use OSS as part of their business, and allow employees to work on OSS projects during their work day. For classic OSS projects that are all-volunteer, why do people contribute? Volunteers are generally self-selected, and care about what they're working on. Benkler (writing in 2002) was building on Raymond's work when he describes the social satisfaction that contributors feel, like I did in porting the button code in MCL. Raymond calls this feeling "egoboo," and describes OSS as "an efficient market in egoboo" (Raymond 1999).

People contribute to OSS projects in many different capacities. A large number of people notice bugs and report them. A well-written bug report is a meaningful contribution! A smaller number of people help fix bugs. An even smaller number contribute major new modules. A study of the Apache web server in 2002 found that although 388 people had contributed code, fifteen of those people wrote 83 percent of the software (Mockus et al. 2002).

One critical innovation of the open software movement is the *release cycle*. Before the wide availability of the internet, software was often delivered to consumers on physical media – CDs or floppy disks. Because sending out a software update via surface mail was expensive and logistically challenging (developers of consumer software didn't necessarily even know who had bought their product), it was critical to meticulously test the code before "going gold" – putting the code on physical media to ship. As a result, the release cycle of software was extremely slow. A game or tool might have just one release, so developers had to be really careful and get it right the first time. This is how it works in the cathedral model.

In contrast, in the bazaar model, Raymond's motto is "release early, release often." If you have the ability to quickly send new versions to everyone using your software via the internet, you can let your users try the software out and effectively be your QA testers. Lots of people testing is a great way to identify problems. Or, as Raymond says, "with enough eyes, all bugs are shallow" (Raymond 1999). Rapid release of new versions of software started in the open software movement and now is the norm for most software development. With easy delivery of software updates, it's no longer necessary to wait until something is perfect (or even really finished) to release it to customers/users. The idea of a "beta version" (a mostly finished version that may have some bugs) or "alpha version" (an early release which is not guaranteed to work well) used to be quite specialized technical jargon, but now are more widely understood.

## Innovation and Leadership in Online Collaboration

Can you innovate in peer production? In many peer production projects, the final outcome is well described at the start of the project. A group of people writing an encyclopedia article about ducks know roughly what that should look like without having to discuss it. Many OSS projects also start with a highly specified goal. Most famously, the Linux operating system is a copy of the UNIX operating system. If you want to contribute to Linux, you can open a UNIX manual and see exactly what your code is supposed to do. This makes collaboration easier, because individuals can jump in and help without having to ask, "What should I do?"

The work process gets more complicated if what you are trying to do is not obvious – if the basic goals or key design decisions need discussion. Doing something everyone already understands can be done with little coordination, in an almost leaderless fashion. Innovating requires some form of leadership.

Is it possible to use volunteer peer production for a complex project where the goal is ill defined? Kurt Luther (then a PhD student, now faculty at Virginia Tech) and I set out to study this question in 2008 (Luther and Bruckman 2011). One interesting example is people who work together to create animations. On the website Newgrounds, people create and share short animated films. Collaborative projects to create animations are called "collabs." We started by interviewing people working on collabs, and wanted to know: How do projects get started, who volunteers, how do people know what to contribute, and who makes the creative decisions?

Like OSS, someone starts a new project on Newgrounds, and that person becomes the benevolent dictator with final creative authority. Animations come in different genres, and it turns out that the type of story (the narrative structure) shapes the work process. For example, one common kind of animation is what we call a "collection." In a collection, the leader asks for short animations on a theme; for example, "when farm animals attack."[4] Contributions are due by a specific date, and must meet requirements like frame rate and length. The task for the leader here is easy. The leader edits the pieces together in a pleasing order, and gets to decide which submissions are included. If someone is late with their contribution or submits something of poor quality, it is not used.

A different kind of animation is a traditional narrative, where you are trying to tell a story. In a narrative, first, someone has to write a script. Next, the script needs to be cut into pieces, each piece assigned to an animator, and a deadline agreed on. If an individual fails to deliver their promised piece by the deadline, the leader has a problem – part of the story is missing. Instead of simply not including

[4] www.newgrounds.com/portal/view/310559.

the late piece as the leader does in a collection, the leader first needs to negotiate with the original animator (are you going to finish this if I give you another two weeks?) and may eventually assign it to someone else. The total workload on the leader is higher, and so is the social stress. In a collection you can simply say, "Sorry, you missed the deadline." The process of leadership for a narrative where each piece is needed is more delicate.

A third common model on Newgrounds is a "continuation." In a continuation, one person starts the animation and hands it off to a second person, who adds the next segment. This allows for a more improvisational type of story-telling – you don't need to script the entire thing in advance. It also fosters aesthetic continuity – when I add my piece, I can make it fit nicely with the piece that came before it. That's harder in a traditional narrative or a collection if animators work in parallel. However, a continuation creates challenges for the leader's efforts to keep the project on time. Instead of working in parallel, creators must work in series. If one person fails to do their part, the whole project comes to a halt.

The key point in these three styles of collab (collection, narrative, and continuation) is that the narrative structure shapes the workflow needed to create it. The structure of the desired product also shapes the time demands and social challenges for a project's leader. More generally, the internal structure of the thing you are making constrains how it can be made.

Most collabs begun on Newgrounds never generate a finished animation. In a quantitative study of these animation projects in 2010, we found that 87.4 percent of projects are never completed (Luther et al. 2010). A major challenge for these projects is that the leader is a bottleneck for all activity. If the leader is overwhelmed by the amount of work, the project slows. If the leader gives up on the project, it dies, and all the work contributed by others goes to waste. Leadership is a critical factor to the success or failure of online creative collaborations.

Notice that the leader of a collab is making the majority of the creative decisions – what to ask people to do, what contributions to accept, and how to integrate the parts. Would it be possible for everyone contributing to the project to have greater overall creative input? To explore this idea, Kurt created a project management tool called Pipeline, specifically designed to support this kind of collaboration. The Pipeline software allows a project leader to post tasks that need to be done and let individuals self-select who will take on each task. When a task is completed, there is a space to discuss that particular contribution. Without Pipeline, people usually send their contribution to the leader, and the leader offers feedback. Pipeline made it easier for everyone on the project team to offer input. In use by animators, artists, and people participating in a creative scavenger hunt, we found that Pipeline helped more members of project teams to have creative input (Gonzales et al. 2015; Luther et al. 2013).

Is it better for more people to have creative input in a collaborative project? That's actually debatable. We have competing clichés: Some would argue that "many hands make light work," while others would say that "too many cooks spoil the broth." Both approaches have advantages for different kinds of projects. In a study of four OSS projects, Nakakoji et al. found that the more exploratory and innovative a project is, the more it benefits from strong top-down leadership (Nakakoji et al. 2002). Whether it's possible to innovate with more peer-to-peer creative control is an intriguing question. There's a lot more interesting research to be done on structures for collaboration and how they shape the final product.

## When Good Will Fails: Boaty McBoatface

Everything we have discussed so far presumes that volunteers are sincerely trying to help, and that volunteers and project organizers share similar goals. Sometimes that's not true. In an amusing example of lack of shared goals, in 2016 the UK government created an online poll to pick the name of a new Arctic research ship. The winning name, by over 100,000 votes, was "Boaty McBoatface." Internet voters saw this as an opportunity for comedy, and didn't share the goal of coming up with a name for the ship that was acceptable to those with more restrained sensibilities. The ship was eventually named the RSS *Sir David Attenborough* (the poll's fifth highest suggestion) (Chappell 2016), but they did use the name "Boaty McBoatface" for three small, yellow, unmanned submersibles it carries (Dwyer 2017). While this story is harmless and amusing, others are less so, as we'll see in Chapter 6 regarding bad content and bad behavior online.

## Theoretical Summary

In peer production, volunteers self-select to perform tasks that match their capabilities and interests. Peer review keeps the quality of contributions high. Allowing people to self-select tasks can help make better use of human creativity and effort.

For volunteers to work together on a project, the work needs to be divisible into small, modular chunks. Having pieces of different sizes lets people participate who have different levels of expertise, interest, and available time. Individual contributions typically need to be integrated into a functioning whole. Easy integration of parts helps support the growth of a project.

Integration of parts is usually accomplished by a project's leaders. Most collaborative projects operate as a benevolent dictatorship where the project's founder has final authority over what pieces are included in the final product. The leader of a collaborative project may become a bottleneck if they have too much work to do in support of the project. Better-designed tools can help lower the leader's workload.

In most peer production systems, a small number of people do most of the work. However, short-time participants also play a significant role. Organizers of online collaborative projects need both to recruit new members to participate (designing for initial motivation), and encourage some members to stay and become regular contributors (designing for sustained engagement).

While many collaborative projects require extremely simple contributions from volunteers, it is possible to organize projects where the group does something more complex, like making an animated movie, uncovering the structure of a protein, or proving a mathematical theorem. The structure of a collaboration shapes both the work process and the nature and quality of the product.

## Practical Implications

What's the next big thing that volunteers, working together, can accomplish? Looking at the structure of existing successful projects, we can begin to understand what is easy and what is hard. Peer production can help us make better use of human creativity and human effort. Most people contribute to these projects both for the satisfaction of contributing to something meaningful, and because it's fun. The challenge for designers is to invent new ways to allow people to participate.

So far I've touched briefly on the question of the *quality of the results* of peer production. As we have seen, data from crowdsourced projects like citizen science can be highly accurate and scientifically valid, if the project is well designed and managed. In the next chapter, I will tackle the most controversial and often poorly understood question regarding the validity of peer-produced content: Should you believe Wikipedia?

# 3    Should You Believe Wikipedia?

In the previous chapter, I explored how Wikipedia works. But is it any good? Should you believe what you read on Wikipedia? My children's middle- and high-school teachers all forbid students from citing it, and some ask that they not use it at all. Are they right? To answer that question, we need first to back up and ask a bigger question: How do we know anything at all?

## How Do You Know?

Do you believe that human activity is changing our global climate? One way or the other, how do you know? I walked around my department one morning asking that question. One person said she knew climate change was real because "scientific data supports it." I asked, "Have you actually read any papers on the topic?" Paraphrasing, here are the answers I got:

- "I've read abstracts of a few scientific studies and heard reports on the science on news sources I trust."
- "I read one study all the way through, and beyond that heard about it on the news."
- "I've never actually read any climate science, but I've heard news reports."
- "They taught us about it in sixth grade."

- "I saw Al Gore's movie."
- "I took a trip to Alaska recently. We had to walk two hours to get to the glacier. They told me that just a few years ago, the glacier was right there – you didn't have to walk to get to it at all."

All my colleagues believe climate change is real. None of them are actually climate scientists. In the absence of enough time to really study the issue, they rely on sources they trust. But what about the other side – the people who do not believe that human activity is changing our climate? How have they come to that conclusion?

For the sake of argument, let's take as a given that human activity is really changing the climate – climate change is real. Is the other side simply delusional? Have we entered the "post-truth" era? "Post-truth" was the word of the year for 2016, according to the Oxford Dictionaries. It is defined as "relating to or denoting circumstances in which objective facts are less influential in shaping public opinion than appeals to emotion and personal belief" (Oxford Dictionaries 2016). This perspective implies there are thoughtful people who rely on facts, and careless people who don't. It's certainly true that some people are intellectually careless (we can't tell how many), but I will argue that this view fails to describe what is taking place in a useful way. It's not that one side is relying on sources and the other is not – both sides have sources. Unless you are a true expert on a given topic, the best you can do is rely on sources you trust. The problem then becomes: *How do you decide which sources to trust?*

Information overload and the complexity of modern life mean that we don't have time to make truly informed decisions on most issues. I don't have time to get a graduate degree in either climate science or immunology – I need quicker ways than that to decide whether it is worth paying extra money to buy a low-emissions car, and whether it is safe to vaccinate my children. So I rely on sources I trust. Each person's decisions about which sources to trust are somewhat mysterious. In a bygone era, people were told what to believe on important matters by community and religious leaders. In contemporary times those decisions are often shaped by mass media (starting with the inventions of print, radio, and television), and more recently by the internet and social media.

If we now assume that climate change is debatable, how can we have that debate? For example, suppose we ask, "Should I believe Al Gore's movie?"[1] The next logical step would be to find the sources that support the film. But then we need to find the sources for those sources – and on *ad infinitum*. Is there any kind of "base fact" that is beyond dispute that we can then build on? This is a question of *epistemology*, the theory of knowledge. If we now ask, "Why do some people choose to believe Al Gore's movie, and others don't?" that is a question of *sociology of knowledge*.

On most issues, people are predisposed to believe a certain way, and therefore accept sources that agree. This is called "confirmation bias" (Nickerson 1998). On the internet, there are sources to support every possible point of view.

[1] *An Inconvenient Truth*, https://en.wikipedia.org/wiki/An_Inconvenient_Truth

If you believe that humanity is arrogant and we have not been good stewards of our natural resources, then you are more inclined to believe that climate change is real and read the *Huffington Post*. If you believe that humanity has been divinely given dominion over the earth and natural resources are there expressly for our use, then you are more inclined to believe that climate change is not real and read *Breitbart*. Each worldview has a set of ideas that are easily assimilated and ideas that don't seem to fit. The internet helps create new worldviews, with sources to support them and other people who believe them. Those groups – whether they have typical or atypical views – support one another's beliefs.

Those worlds are increasingly isolated. When I walked around my office building asking about climate change, I couldn't find a single person who had doubts. Or if they did, they were not comfortable admitting it. Social worlds foster views of reality, and those social worlds these days sometimes don't overlap in any harmonious way.

People who do and do not believe in climate change use similar methods to decide what to believe – media and human sources they trust. But that does not mean that both sides are "right." A preponderance of evidence suggests climate change is real – there is a "true" answer. How do I know? Because I am willing to assert that my sources (high-quality journalism and peer-reviewed scientific publications) are more robust than competing sources.

What does it mean for something to be "true"? How is the internet changing how we understand truth? This chapter explores how theories of the nature of truth and knowledge can help us to understand the internet.

Of course, one could spend a lifetime trying to truly understand these questions (and many people do). Here I will simply give a high-level introduction to parts of these theories I have found helpful as an internet user and researcher.

## Metaphysics: Internal Realism

Everything we know, we experience through our senses. Our senses are fallible. We can make mistakes in what we perceive, and every observation has a limit to its accuracy.

With our fallible senses, we create representations of the world – both internal (mental) ones and external ones (writing, maps, etc.). Those representations are always approximate. When I was studying high-school physics, I thought that we were working with approximate models of situations, because we were just in high school – later we would learn the "real" solutions. As an undergraduate physics major, I quickly learned that all solutions would always be approximations. The models get more and more sophisticated, but they are always approximations. As Jorge Luis Borges wrote, the only perfect map of the territory is the territory itself (Borges and Hurley 1999). The universe is, atom for atom, a perfect model for itself – and anything else has some degree of error in representation.

To further complicate things, the act of observation changes the thing being measured. Sometimes that difference is significant, and sometimes not. It's clearly significant in the subatomic realm, where bouncing a photon off of a particle to observe it moves the particle. It's also clear in the social realm, where, for example, the presence of an observer shapes an individual's behavior. Erving Goffman wrote about how humans are always performing for others, trying to make a particular impression (Goffman 1959). The impressions given (what we intend to communicate) may be different from the impressions given off (what others actually infer from our performance) (more on this in Chapter 5). In many other cases, the act of observation is less significant.

If all I know is what my senses tell me, how do I know I'm not dreaming? How do I know that the world exists at all? This is a question of metaphysics. An objectivist view argues that the world exists and we can reliably know things about it. A subjectivist view argues that we are trapped within the limitations of our senses and cannot definitively know anything.

Much ink has been spilled debating objectivist versus subjectivist views of reality. Fortunately, there is a common-sense compromise called "internal realism." How do I know the world exists? Honestly, I don't. But statistically, it's highly likely. I am trapped within my subjective perceptions and the limitations of my senses. You are trapped within yours. But let's suppose that we both agree that I am sitting on a chair. If our perceptions are so fallible, why do we agree? Now let's suppose I ask the hundred or so people who work in this building to come by and offer their opinions, and everyone agrees that I am sitting on a chair. The reason that we all agree is that *the chair exists*. I can't prove it, but the high degree of correlation between our subjective perceptions leads me to believe that the world is real, independent of my perceptions of it. This philosophical approach was first articulated by Hilary Putnam (Lakoff 1987). The world exists, but is only knowable through the fallible senses of people who are part of the world (not separate from it). The limits of our senses and the fact that we are part of the world we are observing both lead to limits on the accuracy of what we can claim "is true."

## Epistemology

The world exists, but through our limited point of view and fallible senses, what can we know about it? What does it mean to know something? Epistemology is the study of knowledge. To know something, you must believe it, it must be true, and your belief must be justified (Steup 2016). If I am a contestant on a game show and I say, "I know the grand prize is behind door number three!" that is not know-ledge, even if I happen to be right. My belief (though correct) was not justified. On the other hand, if I am a stagehand and saw the grand prize behind door number three, then I have knowledge (true, justified belief) that the prize is there. I know because I saw it with my senses. One candidate for a justified belief is something we directly perceive with reliable senses.

How do we decide whether a belief is justified? Epistemologists debate the nature of justification, and whether justification is necessary or makes sense at all. Two basic approaches to justification are evidentialism and reliabilism. Evidentialism says beliefs must be supported by evidence – all beliefs can be derived from a set of justified, basic beliefs. Basic beliefs include things you learn through reliable senses, and spontaneously formed beliefs if they are a "proper response to experience" (Feldman 2003). Non-basic beliefs are formed by inference from basic ones. In this view, it's challenging to know anything if we have to follow a chain of evidence all the way down to basic beliefs.

On the other hand, reliablism suggests that a belief is reliable if it is the result of a reliable cognitive process. A reliable process is one that generally leads to correct outcomes. Richard Feldman provides the example of two bird-watchers:

> Compare a novice bird-watcher and an expert walking together in the woods, seeking out the rare pink-spotted flycatcher. A bird flies by and each person spontaneously forms the belief that there is a pink-spotted flycatcher there. The expert knows this to be true but the novice is jumping to a conclusion out of excitement. The expert has a well-founded belief but the novice does not. (Feldman 2003, 75)

Having a truly reliable process can be a challenge. The theory of *virtue epistemology* argues that obtaining know-ledge is *an achievement*. Knowledge is the result of "competent cognitive agency" (Greco 2021). Epistemic virtues include "curiosity, intellectual autonomy, intellectual humility, attentiveness, intellectual carefulness, intellectual thoroughness, open-mindedness, intellectual courage and intellectual tenacity" (Heersmink 2017). Critically, obtaining knowledge is not usually something you do by yourself – it is a social process. Knowledge is the result of successful collaboration.

When are you justified in believing something because someone else told you? In epistemology, this is the problem of *testimony*. By accepting someone's testimony, you make yourself vulnerable to possibly accepting bad information either because of their ignorance or dishonesty. The problem of testimony comes down to deciding who to trust.

If testimony that you accept is correct, you are collaboratively building knowledge. To explain how testimony is collaborative, John Greco draws an analogy to a soccer pass:

> Soccer: Playing in a soccer game, Ted receives a brilliant, almost impossible pass. With the defense out of position and goalie lying prostrate on the ground, Ted kicks the ball into the net for an easy goal. (Greco 2021, 96)

The goal is a collaborative achievement between the midfielder and our striker, Ted. In this example, most of the credit goes to the midfielder, but it's definitely a collaborative effort. Greco argues that gaining knowledge through testimony is similar. If all goes well, it is a collaborative achievement of the speaker and the listener. Further, the social environment shapes whether successful knowledge transmission is likely to take place. Greco writes that "In cases of knowledge transmission, the reliability of the testimonial exchange is at least partly explained by the social environment. More exactly, it is explained (in part) by the social norms that structure the social environment, and the ways hearer and speaker sensibilities interact with those norms" (Greco 2021, 78).

These ideas from epistemology give us new ways of understanding the internet. When we receive information online, we can ask: Am I justified in accepting this as true?

Justified because of evidence I have direct access to or because it comes from a reliable source?

Receiving information from someone else online (like a post on social media) is an attempt at creating knowledge through testimony. Reliability of the testimonial exchange is determined by features of the environment (the social media platform) and social norms for people contributing content there. The design of the platform shapes whether the result is likely to be knowledge (true, justified belief) or not. Internet users can pay attention to features of platforms to help them decide what to believe. Designers of platforms have an important job: to design to facilitate the successful creation of knowledge.

## Social Construction of Knowledge

The fact that everyone in the Technology Square Research Building agrees that I am sitting on a chair led me to the qualified statement that it is highly likely that there is such a thing as "a chair" and I am sitting on one. More broadly, that's a pretty good metaphor for how science works. In 1908, Robert Millikan and Harvey Fletcher did an experiment with oil drops and concluded that the charge on an electron is unitary – depending on how many electrons you have, the charge is all in multiples of the same base number (Holton 1978). At the time, that was a controversial claim. Today, we would say "Millikan was right." How do we know? We know because more than 100 years of subsequent scientific research confirms that finding.

Millikan made some observations and drew conclusions – but he might've been wrong. In fact, his experiment was controversial because his original notes have some anomalous findings in the margins. Next to numbers that do not fit his theory are comments like, "Very low. Something wrong," and "Possibly a double drop" (Holton 1978, 70). Those oil drops were not included in the final analysis. Did he cheat, and throw away data that didn't match what he wanted to find? Historian of science Gerald Holton argues that there was probably something observably different about those drops that made Millikan throw out the data points (Holton 1978). In our naive everyday understanding of science, measurement is a precise process and the things we measure either support or disprove our hypotheses. In reality, every step of the process can be messy and require active interpretation – struggling to decide whether to exclude possible double drops is the norm rather than the exception.

Science is a messy process, and it is only through verification of results over time that we can judge which findings are "true." Bruno Latour and Stephen Woolgar document the ways in which the acceptance of a new scientific fact is inherently social (Latour et al. 1986). In the field of science studies, this approach is called *constructivism*. At first, in the written scientific literature, it appears as a qualified claim: Millikan and Fletcher claim that the charge on the electron is unitary. As more people duplicate the finding and more people accept it, it might appear with a citation: "since the charge on the electron is unitary (Millikan 1909) ..." As it becomes even more broadly accepted, the citation drops out. One can simply refer to the concept without citation because it is broadly accepted as "true." The need to attribute an idea falls away as the idea is accepted by more people. The process of something being accepted by the scientific community is social.

Of course, sometimes the process of creating social consensus makes mistakes. When my father, Robert Bruckman, first started practicing orthopedic surgery, it was standard practice to apply heat to certain kinds of injuries and cold to others. At some point, the recommendation changed to always use cold. He jokes, "In around the mid-1970s, there was a spontaneous change in the human body, making it more responsive to cold than heat." Before the mid-1970s, it was "true" that applying heat is sometimes a good idea. After the 1970s, it was no longer true. Of course the human body didn't suddenly change – we were wrong about what was best. The process of learning that we are wrong is also social. Anything that we agree "is true" might be wrong. But what we agree is true at any given moment is our best attempt.

Here we get into a philosophical nuance: When someone said heat is good for some injuries, were they "wrong"? Later evidence suggests it. But at the time, we didn't know. Constructivists like Latour and Woolgar argue that objective truth does not exist independent of a human in a social context who knows that truth at a particular moment in time. Social epistemologists argue that whether we are confused about it or not, objective truth exists (Goldman 1999). I agree with the social epistemologists and Putnam's internal realism – truth exists but we have only indirect access to it (Lakoff 1987). The distinction is subtle, but important. Regardless, for practical purposes, the best we can say is that all knowledge is contingent. Saying something "is true" is linguistic shorthand for, "evidence strongly suggests it, and this is the best we can do until we learn otherwise."

## Peer Review

If truth is socially constructed, how does establishing it work in practice? Peer review is the main mechanism in scientific communities. A finding is reduced to written form as a paper, and that paper is reviewed by experts in the field. The credibility of a paper depends on the rigor of the review process it underwent. Peer review is a way to operationalize social construction of knowledge.

In practice, how carefully something is reviewed depends on the type of publication it has been submitted to. Journal articles are typically the highest standard. Papers submitted to high-quality journals are sent to three experts in the field, and experts review and re-review versions of the paper until it is approved. Reviewers are typically anonymous, to encourage them to be honest. In some fields, review of conference papers is comparable in rigor to journal articles. In my areas of expertise (human–computer interaction and social computing), conference publications are arguably now more important than journals. In many fields (particularly in the humanities), conference publications are lightly reviewed or not reviewed at all and serve as a way to get feedback from peers on ideas in progress.

We discuss this topic in the undergraduate class I teach on "Computing, Society, and Professionalism," and it always surprises my students to learn that books are typically less carefully reviewed than other publications. Undergraduate textbooks and books in some humanities disciplines are carefully reviewed, but in other disciplines the review can be cursory. A book manuscript may get comments from a few experts in the field or may not, and the author and publisher are free to ignore comments they don't agree with. People who review book manuscripts may be anonymous, but often are known to the author, which encourages people to err on the side of being diplomatic rather than frank.

Newspaper articles and magazines go through a different form of pre-publication review: fact-checking. High-quality publication venues have staff assigned to make sure everything they publish is correct. This is both to protect the publication's reputation as reliable, and also to prevent lawsuits for libel. As economic models to support journalism have eroded, many publications no longer fact check or do so less.

Lots of online information receives no formal review. Anyone can put up a blog post or post on an online discussion site and say whatever they like. Some sites support comments or up and down votes, which provide some feedback on the content. However, those are not equivalent to formal review.

## The Reality of Review

It's important not to idealize the process of peer review. Even for a top journal, it's not always what you expect. As research has gotten more inter-disciplinary, it becomes harder for a reviewer to truly understand all the research literature that a new publication is building on. Reviewing is a social process. An editor or conference program committee member requests that others review something. The request typically goes to someone they know. In deciding whether to accept the request, the potential reviewer considers a host of factors, including whether they are interested in the topic, whether they understand the area well enough, and whether they owe the requester a favor (did he/she recently review something for me?). Once in the middle of reviewing, the reviewer typically finds parts of the work they understand thoroughly, and other parts that are more unfamiliar. I will include comments for the editor explaining what parts I know better, and what parts I know less well. It's the editor's job to make sure that at least one person is an expert on each aspect of the paper, but sometimes that is not how it turns out.

If something I am reviewing cites something I haven't read, should I go read it? In theory I should (and occasionally I do), but it's simply not possible to do that as a matter of standard practice. Given the number of things I'm expected to review and the number of citations each of those contains, I often have to assume that the reference says what the authors say it says. Which is by no means assured.

Ole Bjorn Rekdal (2014) tells the story of the birth of an "academic urban legend" – the idea that spinach is a good dietary source of iron (which is not true). Sloppy failure to check citations perpetuated the myth for decades. Realizing this, a paper by K. Sune Larsson in 1995 wrote that "The myth from the 1930s that spinach is a rich source of iron was due to misleading information in the original publication: a malpositioned decimal point gave a 10-fold overestimate of iron content (Hamblin 1981)" (Larsson 1995, 448–449). You would think that someone debunking an error in the scientific literature would themselves be careful; however, it turns out that Hamblin had no support for the story of the decimal point and there is no evidence to suggest that really happened (Rekdal 2014). The story about the origin of an academic urban legend is itself an academic urban legend!

Before you read this chapter, did you believe spinach was a good source of iron? Before I read Rekdal's account, I certainly did. The myth of the iron content of spinach spread and was perpetuated in a community of scientists working in peer-reviewed publications. In this case, the mechanisms to stop such errors (scientific training and peer review) failed. If it's possible for scientists publishing in journals to create such a persistent falsehood, imagine how easy it is for untrained individuals sharing non-peer-reviewed information on the internet to create falsehoods that are stubbornly hard to kill.

## Should You Believe Wikipedia?

As we have seen, the reliability of a publication depends on its degree of review. I will argue that as a result, Wikipedia is sometimes the most reliable publication ever created – and other times not so at all. *It depends on the article.*

Wikipedia can be edited by anyone. Most pages even allow anonymous users to make changes without logging in. Learning that it can be edited by anyone, regardless of their formal qualifications, many people with a traditional bent are repulsed. As we saw in the case of global warming, people are often predisposed to believe a particular way. People who, for example, have a traditional view of authority/credibility are likely to (in the absence of evidence one way or the other) be suspicious of Wikipedia. Those who are inclined to hold positivist, techno-utopian views of the transformative potential of technology are likely (in the absence of evidence) to be excited by it.

The truth is more complicated than it seems on the surface. Consider the case of a really popular article, with many people editing it. Next time someone is nominated to the US Supreme Court or chosen as the new Pope, take a look at their Wikipedia page. If you click on the "history" tab, you can see every past version of an article, and when it was edited. When someone is suddenly elevated from relative obscurity to a position of prominence, you see Wikipedia at its best.

Consider, for example, the page of current US Supreme Court Chief Justice John Roberts. His page was created in May 2005, with a few short paragraphs on his educational and professional background and the fact that he served at that time as a judge on the US Court of Appeals for the District of Columbia (total text of 182 words). The page had nine edits in total until July 19 of that year, when he was nominated to the US Supreme Court. That day, it was edited thirty-one times, and over 1,200 times by the end of July. Edits were made in July by 359 different people (174 logged-in users, the rest anonymous users). As of 2020, the text is over 6,800 words long. In addition to reviewing his biography in detail, it reviews positions he has taken as a judge in detail, and links to separate pages about cases he argued before the Supreme Court before becoming a justice, and separate pages about dozens of decisions he made in previous judgeships. His biography is detailed and supported by reliable citations. If you were to insert a random false statement into the article, it would likely be fixed immediately (Viegas et al. 2004). (Please don't do this!)

As we saw before, refereed journal articles are arguably the "gold standard" for quality of information. However, a refereed journal article is reviewed typically by three experts. How do you compare three experts to hundreds of self-selected volunteers? If the volunteers have no real background in the area, they might be able to improve things like readability, grammar, and formatting, but might not be able to contribute much to the substance of the article. However, what if they have access to an internet full of information about the topic, and can read references carefully?

Any edit on Wikipedia is typically supported by a reputable citation. If someone adds information without a citation, it is usually quickly removed. When every edit has strong evidence behind it, hundreds of volunteers will do better than a few experts.

Many articles on Wikipedia in fact now do draw communities of experts around them. When my children were young, they suffered from serious food allergies. In the mid-2000s there was one article on "food allergy." I created separate articles for some common allergens, including egg, dairy, peanut, and tree-nut allergy. In the early days, I was able to contribute to those articles easily – clarifying details or adding new studies. However, over time the articles have become more specialized, with many contributors with professional expertise. The sophistication of Wikipedia editors has increased over time. I still think I could contribute to the articles if I was careful, and experts are there to catch any mistakes I might make. Once you've edited an article, it is added to your "watch list," and Wikipedia editors often check new changes to articles they care about. Experts and non-experts form an intriguing "community of practice" around each article, as we'll see in Chapter 4.

A journal article goes through the review process once, and then is frozen. If new information emerges to change the consensus view of a phenomenon, subsequent publications can address that, but the original publication doesn't change (it can only be retracted, if it's found to be really wrong). A Wikipedia article can be updated on a moment-by-moment basis. In terms of social construction of knowledge, the more people have reviewed something, the more we can trust it. Hundreds of people continually updating a popular Wikipedia page *arguably creates the most reviewed and up-to-date information source ever created.*

While a popular Wikipedia page is heavily reviewed, a less popular Wikipedia page may have hardly been reviewed at all. For example, the page on the Massachusetts State House was created in 2004, and is edited just a handful of times per year. Sections of the article have a "citation needed" tag, warning readers that the section needs additional citations for verification. The page (as of May 2020) includes text saying:

> Murals on the second floor under the dome were painted by artist Edward Brodney. Brodney won a competition to paint the first mural in a contest sponsored by the Works Progress Administration in 1936. It is entitled "Columbia Knighting Her World War Disabled." Brodney could not afford to pay models, and friends and family posed. The model for Columbia was Brodney's sister Norma Brodney Cohen, and the model for the soldier on one knee in the foreground was his brother Fred Brodney. In 1938, he painted a second mural under the dome called "World War Mothers." The models were again primarily friends and family members, with sister Norma sitting beside their mother Sarah Brodney. The *New York Times* notes that the murals are relatively rare examples of military art with women as their subjects.[2]

If you follow the citations, there is support for the fact that Sarah Brodney was the model for the war mothers, but no support for the statement that Norma was the model for Columbia. I promise it's true – I'm the person who added that text in October 2008. Norma was my grandmother, and Sarah was my great grandmother. I would add a citation if I had one. In 2008, you could sometimes get away with adding an unsourced statement to Wikipedia if it was on a not particularly popular page. Today, it's less likely. Part of the reason that the mention of Norma has stayed is because *no one cares about the Massachusetts*

---

[2] https://en.wikipedia.org/wiki/Massachusetts_State_House#Inside_the_building

*State House*. A low-profile page is much less reliable because it is less carefully reviewed.

Epistemologist Don Fallis notes, "Admittedly, many Wikipedia entries do not get a lot of traffic and, thus, will not be checked frequently for errors. But because they do not get a lot of readers, the potential epistemic cost of errors in these entries is correspondingly lower as well." The system is self-optimizing: The more people are interested in an article, the more reliable it is likely to be (Fallis 2008, 1669–1670).

Other sites often copy text from Wikipedia. A number of other websites now quote the statements about Norma and Fred. Sometimes, this leads to a false citation loop, or "citogenesis" (Frost-Arnold 2018). Here's how this happens. First, someone puts unsourced content on Wikipedia. Next, someone else writes an article and uses Wikipedia as a source without attribution. Next, a Wikipedia editor decides to improve the page by adding better citations, does a web search, finds the article, and adds a citation to it! The appearance of a source is created when in fact there's no support at all. It happens to be true that the models in those murals were Norma and Fred, but if it weren't true, it would be hard to remove that information from the internet. Uneven evaluation of the quality of sources is a weakness of the model.

Separate from the question of whether the contents of an encyclopedia article are true is the question of what it chooses to cover. What topics have articles? Halavais and Lackaff compared the topic of a random sample of Wikipedia articles to representation of those topics in *Books in Print*, and found that it varies – for example, the physical sciences are better represented than the social sciences. Comparing Wikipedia to specialized dictionaries, they found that Wikipedia's coverage of physics and linguistics is better than its coverage of poetry. And of course, topics of general interest like popular culture are disproportionately well covered – there's a whole lot that's been written about Harry Potter and Star Wars (Halavais and Lackaff 2008). Wikipedia's coverage continuously expands, so how well it represents any area is constantly changing (Mesgari et al. 2015).

If an article exists on a topic, how thorough is it? What things are included and what things are left out? Historian Roy Rosenzweig (2006) compared twenty-five biographies on Wikipedia to the same subjects covered in a scholarly work, American National Biography Online (ANBO). Both were reliable – Rosenzweig found four minor factual errors in those twenty-five articles in Wikipedia and one in ANBO. More interesting, though, is differences in the style of the articles and what they choose to include. Comparing the biographies of American president Abraham Lincoln, both are accurate. ANBO has elegant prose, richer contextualization, connections to themes in historiography, and confident judgment. Wikipedia has an explicit policy demanding that articles have a "neutral point of view" (NPOV), so judgment is not allowed. The Wikipedia article was also written by many people, and as a result can't have such flowing prose. However, Wikipedia has many fun, colorful details about Lincoln that are not present in ANBO (like the fact that he shared a birthday with Charles Darwin, or that he wrote the edict to make

Thanksgiving a national holiday in the United States) (Rosenzweig 2006).

In "Towards an Epistemology of Wikipedia," Don Fallis (2008) concludes that Wikipedia is largely reliable, but also reminds us that there are other epistemic virtues beyond reliability – notably "power, speed, and fecundity. That is, we are also concerned with how much knowledge can be acquired from an information source, how fast that knowledge can be acquired, and how many people can acquire that knowledge" (Fallis 2008). Wikipedia excels by those measures.

## Theoretical Summary

It's surprising how much philosophy is needed to answer a simple question – whether you should believe Wikipedia. The underlying philosophical questions, like whether objective truth exists, have no simple answers. My own thinking tends to embrace common-sense, moderate compromises. The view I have cobbled together for myself is, in sum:

> The world exists, but is only knowable through our fallible senses (internal realism). Truth likely exists independent of knowledge and the knower, but we have only human ways of attempting to gain access to it. Because our senses are fallible, the way we determine what we believe "is true" is through social consensus (social epistemology). Social consensus is sometimes wrong, and we are constantly improving on it.
>
> Knowledge requires true, justified belief. Knowledge is an achievement of a reliable cognitive process. Sharing

knowledge is a collaborative achievement, and key features of the social environment shape whether that process is likely to be successful.

Wherever you personally land on these thorny questions, insights from epistemology (what is true) and sociology of knowledge (what people choose to believe) are becoming surprisingly useful on a day-to-day basis. Not just Wikipedia, but the entire internet is a swirling ecosystem of social construction of knowledge in action.

## Practical Implications

Knowing something about the nature of knowledge and truth, what can we do better as users of the internet and designers of internet-based communication systems? At the simplest level, it helps to be aware of the fragility of all knowledge. Epistemologists can debate what a "basic fact" is and what it means for something to be really supported, but on a day-to-day basis none of us have time to dig down into support for ideas until we hit some kind of basic fact bedrock (if such a thing even exists). We are not all climate scientists – if we want to decide whether it's worth extra money to buy a low-emissions car, we need to choose sources we trust. And no one can be knowledgeable about everything – even actual climate scientists need to find sources they trust about whether to vaccinate their kids, eat gluten, or buy produce from genetically modified crops.

Understanding more about social construction and the nature of knowledge, we can be better consumers of information and better designers of information systems.

Consider this example: Recently, I accidentally retweeted a false news story. The story stated that drivers for ride-sharing services Uber and Lyft were making a median profit of $3.37 per hour – shockingly low (Levin 2018). The article was posted by the newspaper the *Guardian* (arguably one of the most reputable news sources in the world), and was based on a study done at MIT (arguably one of the most prestigious research institutions in the world). With that pedigree, I retweeted the story without thinking about it too deeply. Friends on Twitter immediately expressed skepticism – that number can't be right, why would so many people be driving for those services if the pay was so low? Digging deeper, it turns out that the MIT paper was just a working paper – it hadn't undergone peer review. In fact, after criticism from Uber, the MIT authors posted a correction – the median is $8.55 per hour (a much more reasonable figure). I quickly deleted my posting, and tweeted a correction. By posting something false without realizing it, I contributed to the problem of *misinformation*. Sharing something false deliberately is *disinformation*, and I'll talk about that in Chapter 6.

There's bad news and good news in this story. The bad news is that sometimes you can't even trust some of our most hallowed brands, the *Guardian* and MIT. If those information sources aren't always credible, how are we to navigate the sea of articles by much less reputable sources? But the good news is that in this case the system worked. My friends immediately expressed skepticism, and I took down my tweet and posted a correction. The study authors checked their figures and posted a correction. The *Guardian* posted a correction. Viewing this through the lens of an ecology of social construction of knowledge, we can look at what specific design features led to the original error, and what features helped generate a correction.

How do we support people in making well-grounded decisions about what to believe and what to share? One possibility is to provide people with metadata: information on the sources of support for a given piece of information (like the fact that the *Guardian* story was based on a non-peer-reviewed working paper). Many sites have begun efforts to improve in this area. For example, in 2017, Facebook started adding more context to articles (Welch 2018). This includes a link on articles with a small "i" that takes you to a page with the date the article was first shared and a profile of the publisher. This source information is only available on a small fraction of articles, and mainly on articles from major news sources whose reputations are already widely known. It's unfortunately not available where it's needed most – on articles from smaller sites whose reputations may be unclear. In February 2020, Twitter announced that they would start labeling synthetic and manipulated media (Roth and Achuthan 2020). In May 2020, they announced that they would start labeling "potentially harmful and misleading content," particularly related to the coronavirus pandemic (Roth and Pickles 2020), and in late May for the first time marked two tweets by the President of the United States as misleading (Wong and Levine 2020). More and more of his tweets were marked as misinformation over time, until he was finally banned from the platform in January 2021.

Can metadata help? This question leads to a long list of harder questions. Who decides what tweets or articles to mark as misleading or false? By what standard? Assuming the annotation is done well, does marking things as misleading or false help the reader? What design features of the user interface for metadata make it more effective? When does metadata backfire, leading people to be more convinced of the truth of the false claim (Nyhan and Reifler 2016)?

What kinds of meta-information are helpful? How detailed should that information be? How do we generate metadata? Do we use human labor or artificial intelligence to generate it? How do we train the human workers and the algorithms? Do we need multiple sources of metadata, with different underlying values and assumptions? Is there a potential demand for a "reliability service"? Is there a potential business model to support such a service? What approaches other than metadata might help us address the problem of false and misleading information on the internet?

The people struggling with these questions are diverse, including teachers, students, researchers, publishers, and citizens trying to make every possible kind of personal and political decision. We can all make better decisions about what to believe if we are armed with a deeper understanding of the nature of "truth" and "knowledge."

In the next chapter we'll see that part of the problem is who is sharing information with whom – if you don't believe the moon landings actually happened, you are more likely to persist in that belief if you are part of a group who all agree with you (Sunstein 2018).

# 4 How Does the Internet Change How We Think?

US Army company commanders Nate Allen and Tony Burgess became friends at West Point. Living in adjacent houses, they would meet on Allen's front porch in the evenings and share advice. Seeing how much sharing tips helped, in March 2000 they started a website called Company Command. Dan Baum documents their story in his 2005 *New Yorker* article "Battle Lessons, What the Generals Don't Know" (Baum 2005).

As Baum explains, being an army officer can be isolating. He shares the story of Stephanie Gray, a communications officer who was ordered to serve as her battalion's adjutant, administrative assistant to the battalion commander. On her first day, there was a crisis and the leadership of the battalion all rushed to the site. A soldier had been killed. She knew it was her job to process the paperwork, but what was she supposed to do? She posted on Company Command, and got help from people who had done this before. Baum quotes Gray:

> "Within 30 minutes, I got my first response, and all day I got e-mails," she said. "Some were from active military and some retired. One was a chaplain. 'Look at this regulation,' they told me, or 'Here's what I tried.'
> I learned how to report it up, then look in the soldier's file and generate letters from the company commander, the battalion commander, the brigade commanders to his

family ... There were death-benefit papers to fill out, and on and on." (Baum 2005)

How do members of a hierarchical organization share information? Typically in the US military, if an officer has a helpful tip to share with others, they send it up the chain of command. Weeks later, the advice may come back down the chain of command to peers in the form of an advisory. The information is carefully vetted, but transmission is slow. On Company Command, officers could share advice peer-to-peer, in real time. Baum describes how Lieutenant Keith Wilson read an alert online that there were grenades hidden behind posters of Moqtada-el-Sadr being put up in Iraq. Hours later, when Wilson sent his men to take down the posters, one found a grenade behind a poster. If the alert had been sent up and then down the chain of command through the normal process, the information would not have arrived in time.

The most remarkable part of this story is that instead of court marshaling Allen and Burgess for sharing military information on an unsecure, unofficial website, they sent them to get PhDs and continue operating websites for peer-to-peer information sharing!

The kind of communication that takes place on Company Command is called *knowledge-building discourse*. In knowledge-building discourse, a group of people all contribute ideas to try to create new knowledge together. One person contributes a new idea, and others critique it. Over time, the group finds things they agree on, and this is new knowledge. This is ideally what happens in a community of scientists, who build new knowledge through peer review. Internet-based communication tools are particularly good at supporting knowledge-building discourse, because ideas can be shared and critiqued rapidly. Knowledge-building discourse is a process for facilitating the social construction of knowledge.

Knowledge-building discourse changes the kinds of information that people share. Peer-produced information tends to be more *relevant*, because the people who create it share needs and interests with the audience they share it with. It is created more *quickly*, because it doesn't go through formal review. It can be highly reliable if (and only if) significant peer review takes place. Although, as we'll see later in this chapter, peer review sometimes fails. One challenge for people who rely on peer-generated content is (as we saw in Chapter 3) that the level of review is often not immediately apparent to people who are not active participants in the peer-production community.

## Becoming Part of a Knowledge-Building Community

Have you ever contributed to a knowledge-building community? Maybe it was in an online discussion group like a subreddit, a Facebook group, or a mailing list. Think back to when you first joined that group. What did you do initially?

Most people's earliest participation is *lurking* – listening without yet contributing. People lurk to learn the rules and norms of the group, so that they can contribute appropriately when they are ready. Online groups some-times have written rules, like those on a subreddit (Matias 2019), but more often have unwritten ones – things you have to learn by observing. Blair Nonnecke and Jenny Preece studied people who lurk on different kinds of discussion groups, contrasting technical support and health support groups (Nonnecke and Preece 2000). They found that the lurking percentage (the number of people listening but not posting) was dramatically higher for technical support groups – 90 percent of people listened without contributing, compared to 46 percent in health support groups. The reason is that in technical support, questions tend to have objective answers. Once you have that answer, the discussion is usually largely over. That is in contrast to health support, where even when an answer is provided, others may continue to make empathetic remarks and share their own stories. As Nonnecke and Preece point out, lurking is not non-participation – it's a form of participation of its own. We need listeners as well as talkers to make conversations work. Furthermore, the more people who are reading, the more likely it is that someone present will have an answer to a unique or unusual question.

Once a new member lurks for a while, next they typically may participate in some small way. Over time, they slowly participate more deeply, until they are participating in core activities of the group. Lave and Wenger studied this process and described it as "legitimate peripheral participation" (LPP) (Lave and Wenger 1991). A group of people engaged in a goal-directed activity together is a "community of practice." The process of learning to be a part of a community of practice involves moving slowly from the periphery to the center of the group.

In one famous example, Lave and Wenger studied tailors in West Africa. An apprentice tailor starts by sweeping the floor. Their participation is *legitimate*, because the floor needs to be swept. No one is asking the apprentice to do anything for the sole purpose of their training. Their participation is *peripheral* because while they are sweeping the floor, they have the opportunity to observe the practice of the experienced tailors around them. When someone finally asks, "Can you sew this seam?" they have seen it done many times. The process of learning in a community of practice is one of moving from the periphery to the center.

*Visibility of mature practice* is critical to the success of a community of practice as a learning environment. Lave and Wenger present the case of apprentice butchers as an example of failure. The apprentice butchers they observed were asked to wrap meat that had already been cut. However, the wrapping machines were located in a different room than the one in which the experienced butchers work. Consequently, the apprentices never had a chance to observe experienced butchers at work, and were not ready when asked to try the next step (Lave and Wenger 1991, 76–79).

Cognitive work is typically harder to observe than physical work like tailoring and cutting meat. You can see the use of sewing needles and butcher's knives, but it's harder to observe someone doing knowledge work. Collins et al. call the process of learning knowledge work via LPP "cognitive apprenticeship" (Collins et al. 1989). Making the practice of mature members of the community visible is key to the success of knowledge work. It helps if new members can see people expressing ideas, getting feedback, and revising ideas. In online interaction, sometimes cognitive work is in fact made quite visible. New members of a group can see contributions made by more experienced members, begin by making small comments or corrections, and progress to making bigger contributions. In other words, they can learn by LPP.

In 2005, then-students Andrea Forte and Susan Bryant and I set out to interview early contributors to Wikipedia who had become committed editors (Bryant et al. 2005). We wanted to know: Who are these people who are contributing to Wikipedia, and why do they do it? The users we spoke to initially began editing an article they had a strong personal interest in, and made a minor change. For example, one told us, "One of the first things I looked up was Wales, and I found what was already there about Wales, where I live ... I thought, 'Well that's wrong. I'll change that.' And I thought, 'What can I put to make it a bit longer, because it's short.' And then it just sort of ... I just got into the habit really" (Bryant et al. 2005, 4). Over time, our subjects were able to observe the work of others contributing to the community, and gradually take on more complex tasks themselves. As they moved from the periphery to the center of the community, they began to use more sophisticated editing tools, and to see Wikipedia as a community and not just a collection of articles. In other words, becoming a regular Wikipedia editor is a process of LPP in a knowledge-building community of practice! When we started our research, we did not expect it to fit so neatly into our theoretical categories. (I remember joking with Forte at the time, "It's almost as if we make you read all that theory *for a reason*.")

## Knowledge Building as a Socio-technical System

So far we've seen how people think in new ways in a knowledge-building community – compared to traditional approaches, the process of knowledge creation is typically faster and content created is more relevant, but its reliability can vary dramatically. Features of the internet environment help this kind of activity to thrive. For example, the ability for users to upvote and downvote content on some platforms can draw greater attention to content that the group agrees is higher quality. Moderation (both human and automatic) can remove content that is inappropriate before many people see it. The work of knowledge creation is accomplished by a combination of people, social practices, and tools – a socio-technical system.

In fact, you can argue that "the thing that is thinking" as we create new knowledge in a knowledge-building community is not an individual person, but the entire socio-technical system. The act of thinking is distributed across all those human and non-human elements. Edwin Hutchins called this view "distributed cognition" (or "dcog"). Hutchins did a detailed analysis of how cognition is distributed in things like steering an aircraft carrier or landing an airplane (Hutchins 1995a, 1995b). His paper "How a Cockpit Remembers Its Speeds" tells the story of two pilots landing an airplane. The two pilots and the gauges and dials and even small pieces of cardboard (landing cards that show the desired speeds for a given airplane weight) together are all critical to a safe landing. We could say that the two pilots are landing the plane using the tools they've been given and rules they've learned, but Hutchins makes a conceptual shift to say *the entire system is what is doing the thinking.*

A dcog point of view provides an interesting perspective on online conversation. From this perspective, it is the entire socio-technical system that is proving a theorem on the Polymath Projector or creating a verified dataset about galaxies on Zooniverse. Things that shape the outcome include the people, software tools used, division of labor, formal written rules of participation, and unwritten social norms. Similarly, the entire socio-technical system of, for example, a Facebook group is shaping the outcome of the conversation, and differences in all elements of the system shape how a discussion on a Facebook group might be quite different from discussion of the same topic on a subreddit or on Twitter.

## Across Distance

Company Commanders Burgess and Allen lived next door to each other, and benefited greatly from the ease with which they could share ideas and advice. The website they created brought that same benefit to other Company Commanders stationed around the world. The ability of the internet to bring people together independent of geography is transformative.

Consider, for example, people with a rare disease. I have a mild form of the eye disease keratoconus, which causes irregular thinning of the cornea. I have only one friend who also suffers from keratoconus. There might be other people I know who also have keratoconus, but how would I know? It doesn't often come up in conversation. On Reddit, the discussion group r/keratoconus as of January 2021 has 8,100 members. Members share their personal stories, send updates on new research developments, and ask for advice and information. Groups with self-selected membership help people with unique interests, needs, or beliefs to find one another. Those groups can even organize to request changes from government or corporations. People on the website Patients Like Me have gathered research data on their own conditions that was scientifically valid and valuable (PatientsLikeMe 2018).

Bringing people together who have shared interests, needs, values, and assumptions is usually a benefit to them and to society. Usually, but not always.

## Echo Chambers

As we have seen, the quality of peer-produced content depends on the quality of peer review. On Wikipedia, that quality is surprisingly good for a popular page (see Chapter 3). You might think that a page on a controversial topic like vaccines or climate change is likely to be a battle-ground and end up as a mix of information and misinfor-mation; however, a crew of dedicated editors who believe in standards of peer-reviewed science keep these articles surprisingly accurate and free of misinformation. These pages work because lots of people are watching.

What happens when a self-selected group of reviewers all share a strong point of view and reinforce one another's beliefs? This is an *echo chamber* (Sunstein 2018). In traditional publishing, content is vetted by a small number of experts. In knowledge-building communities, a larger number of people with varying expertise review content. In an echo chamber, all the potential reviewers already agree on a set of assumptions, so there may be limited chance to critique those assumptions.

Echo chambers are not inherently bad. They are necessary and useful in lots of situations. For controversial topics, it can be difficult to have any conversation at all if participants don't share certain assumptions. The case of the USENET discussion groups about feminism is an intriguing example. USENET was one of the earliest online discussion forums (pre-dating the World Wide Web).[1] Created in 1980, discussion on USENET was divided into groups like Reddit is today. Groups were in different hierarchies – soc for social science, rec for recreation, sci for science, etc. For example, rec.pets.cats was a discussion group about cats. The process of creating a group involved public discussion and voting. Someone had to propose the new group, its name, and its rules. However, there was one special set of groups in the alt ("alternative") hierarchy that did not require voting – anyone could just create a group and it would appear instantly. (This led to lots of fun and

---

[1] https://en.wikipedia.org/wiki/Usenet

silly groups like alt.swedish.chef.bork.bork.bork and alt.sexy. bald.captains.)

USENET had at least two groups for discussion of feminism: soc.feminism and alt.feminism. USENET content started being archived in 1995 by Deja News, which in 2001 was acquired by Google.[2] Old USENET groups still exist on Google Groups, though they are mostly inactive. When USENET was still active, I used to assign students in my "Design of Online Communities" class to look at both groups and think about why they are different. The group soc.feminism was moderated, and for a post to be approved it had to conform to a set of assumptions about feminism. On the other hand, alt.feminism was unmoderated. As you might guess, the moderated group contained civil discussion of feminist ideas and the unmoderated one was a flame fest. You can still go on Google Groups and see USENET content from the 1990s. Picking a random day (December 31, 1999), posts on alt.feminism offer nude pictures of celebrities, and a discussion "'Feminism as Bigotry' by Daphne Patal." Posts from that same day on soc.feminism include topics like "An Inspiration: Women of Courage" and "Follow up to the Beauty Myth."

The moderated group soc.feminism was an early online echo chamber. If you accept the tenets of feminism and wish to have a thoughtful and civil discussion of the implications, it was perfect. Such discussion was not possible on the unmoderated, alt version of the group. Echo chambers are often valuable and needed.

---

[2] https://en.wikipedia.org/wiki/Google_Groups

However, echo chambers have downsides. In the feminism example, if you have doubts about how statistics about the wage gap are calculated and want to debate the details, you probably would not have been welcome on soc. feminism. People in the echo chamber have a safe space to move further within a particular worldview, but are not likely to be exposed to critiques of that worldview. They are insulated from attacks on their basic assumptions, and that can be constructive – you can't make progress in a conversation if you continually have to defend the fundamentals. However, they are also isolated from legitimate criticisms. The tendency of people in echo chambers to not consider reasonable challenges to their ideas is a key problem for the internet today.

It's important to have different spaces for different kinds of discussions, and different sets of assumptions. However, the current affordances of internet technology have led to an unfortunate polarization. There are plenty of spaces that reaffirm strong positions on issues on both sides, but fewer where people who disagree can meaningfully engage with the nuances of their positions. An interesting counter-example is the subreddit r/NeutralPolitics, which describes itself as "a heavily moderated community dedicated to evenhanded, empirical discussion of political issues. Based on facts and respectful discussion." Their heavy moderation is largely successful in creating a more thoughtful discussion with a civil tone and assertions supported by evidence. We need more spaces that strive for neutrality.

Where we get into serious trouble is when echo chambers have strongly shared assumptions that are *wrong*.

As we saw in Chapter 3, we cannot shy away from sometimes declaring some ideas to be wrong. The earth is a sphere, the Holocaust happened, and vaccines do not cause autism. Unfortunately, the same affordances of online knowledge-building communities that saved Lieutenant Wilson's squad member from a grenade by warning him in time can also help convince people of things that are objectively false.

## Threats to Knowledge Building

The success of collaborative knowledge building depends on contributors' willingness to invest time, knowledge, understanding of the nature of evidence, and sincerity. Each of these elements can fail. If few people contribute, then the collaborative product may not be revised enough to become reliable. This, for example, happens in the case of an obscure Wikipedia page that few people have edited. If participants start with false basic beliefs and assumptions, then the things they infer as a result may be entirely wrong. We saw in Chapter 3 that beliefs are built up from basic beliefs. If you start from false premises, the things you conclude using that as a base will be unreliable. Worse, if some contributors are deliberately trying to harm the final product, then we're really in trouble. (I spent the first twenty years of my career believing that most people on the internet are sincerely trying to help, and I'll spend the next twenty years laughing at myself for being so naive!)

As we saw in Chapter 3, knowledge is socially constructed. What the community of scientists agree on is our best attempt at what "is true," and is continually revised over time in response to new evidence. When we train scientists, we teach them standards for evidence and how to create new scientific knowledge by building on and critiquing existing scientific knowledge. Advancing scientific knowledge is a *social process* that takes place in a community – the community of scientists. We have invented mechanisms like scientific journals, peer review, and scientific conferences to help this social process along and create opportunities for exchange of ideas and advancing the state of knowledge. Increasingly, these same mechanisms are possible to implement for other groups – like people who believe the earth is flat.

Throughout human history, some people have always had what we would call "non-standard beliefs." Sometimes those beliefs even prove to be right! The internet is particularly good at fostering non-standard beliefs, because people who share assumptions can find one another. In the 1950s, it was easy to have a few hundred people receive a flat earth newsletter. In the early twenty-first century, thousands of people or more can easily not only receive a newsletter, but talk to one another on a daily basis, regardless of how far apart they live in the physical world. There are multiple online forums for believers in a flat earth, including useful resources and discussion boards. Videos hosted on YouTube explaining the flat earth are particularly persuasive. Many flat earthers trace the origin of their belief in a flat earth back to watching a compelling video (Sample 2019).

Since at least around 600 BC, science has known that the earth is a sphere.[3] Periodically, a contrarian voice

---

[3] https://en.wikipedia.org/wiki/Spherical_Earth

emerges to declare that the earth is flat, and ideas about a round earth are part of a worldwide conspiracy. In the nineteenth century, Samuel Rowbotham adopted the pseudonym "Parallax," and began traveling Europe giving lectures explaining that the earth is flat. He called his field of inquiry "zetetic astronomy." Parallax grounded his arguments in a literal interpretation of the Judeo-Christian Bible. Christine Garwood writes:

> By claiming to defend the Bible against science, and setting the two in irresolvable conflict, he was bound to attract an audience willing to pay to hear such ideas. In addition, his emphasis on democratic fact-finding could potentially attract self-educated working men, while experimental proofs would gain further authority and credibility for his cause. So, under a banner of power to the people and to the Bible, Parallax sought to mobilize public support. Questions remain about whether Parallax truly believed his own theory. (Garwood 2007, 45)

Parallax made money from his lectures and publications, and it's unclear to what extent he truly believed the earth is flat. His stated motivations were a mix of religion and his version of "science." To prove the earth is flat, all you need to do is conduct an experiment to measure the curvature of the earth, and do it *badly*. Nineteenth-century flat earthers staged dramatic demonstrations of such "proofs" (Garwood 2007). Their rhetoric is fascinating, because they claim to be more scientific than the general population. In their view, they are conducting their own experiments and trusting the evidence of their eyes, while the rest of us are guilty of naively simply believing what we are told.

Parallax was just the first in a long line of promoters of the theory that the earth is flat. In the twentieth century, groups including the International Flat Earth Research Society (IFERS) and the Flat Earth Society of Canada were founded, with a mix of people approaching the subject seriously and ironically (Garwood 2007). As of January 2021, on the website Meetup (which organizes face-to-face meetings of local groups) over 1,900 people in twenty-six local groups are currently registered for flat earth groups around the world (www.meetup.com/topics/flat-earth). Five hundred attended a convention in 2017 (Welch 2017), and 650 in 2018 (Ingold 2018). The website www.theflatearthsociety.org says that it had a high of 3,720 users online at one time on June 17, 2017, according to server statistics on their forum page.

Scientists advance their knowledge by having professional conferences, discussion forums, and publications. Flat earthers *use all these same mechanisms*. Together, they reinforce one another's beliefs. Collectively, they engage in knowledge-building discourse. For example, in one thread on the forum tfes.org (https://forum.tfes.org/index.php?topic=11467.0), flat earthers debate a conundrum: How is it possible that there are sometimes shadows cast on the top of Mount Everest? They begin with assumptions that the earth is flat, Mount Everest is higher than any of the mountains around it, and the sun is always higher up in the sky than the top of Everest. Starting from these premises, the shadow is a conundrum. Participants in the discussion draw diagrams showing light sources and shadows, and photographs of experiments done at home with objects casting shadows. They draw analogies, discussing shadows from street lamps.

Members debate whether the concept of perspective is relevant, or does it just complicate the issue? They cite sources, going back to nineteenth-century writings by Samuel Rowbotham. It's a detailed and thoughtful discussion that looks a whole lot like what we call "science," except that it's starting from false premises.

## Is the Internet Encouraging Belief in Conspiracies?

In fall 2018, Georgia Tech master's student Sijia Xiao and I set out to answer the question: Is the internet encouraging people to believe conspiracy theories? We chose one particular conspiracy theory to study: chemtrails. People who adopt the chemtrails conspiracy believe that the condensation trails visible behind airplanes are deliberately sprayed for nefarious purposes. Some believe that the trails are for climate control, and others that they are for deliberate depopulation. We set out to interview chemtrails believers, and ask them how they came to know about chemtrails, focusing in particular on trying to understand the role of the internet.

Xiao had surprisingly little difficulty finding people who would talk with her. Many believers are passionate about chemtrails and eager to share what they know. We even received an email from a staff member at our transcription service, saying:

> Your work is so important! I want to tell you more about what I know about this topic. I know I could get fired from my job for contacting you, so I am contacting you from an anonymous account.

We declined to contact this person further. All in all, we interviewed twenty-eight people, including a mix of believers in chemtrails (thirteen) and other conspiracies, and also debunkers who spend time trying to convince people not to believe. To our surprise, we met a group of ex-believers (seven) who could share with us both why they initially believed and what changed their minds.

Although everyone's belief journey is different, many research subjects told us that YouTube videos played a central role in forming their initial beliefs in chemtrails:

> The convenience about YouTube is very easy to go and have a look at someone's video that they've already put together. All the information, they've bundled it together, sugar coated it, and made it really nice and fluffy packaged. (Believer)
>
> When you watch the videos, and I know how to look out for this now, but they use music, and stuff to, they use fear and music to manipulate your emotions. (Ex-believer)

Intriguingly, Asheley Landrum found the same thing more strongly in her study of flat earthers: Every flat earther she spoke with had first learned about the flat earth on YouTube (Landrum et al. 2019; Sample 2019).

Once people learn about chemtrails, many join Facebook groups for chemtrails believers. Members of these groups reinforce one another's beliefs, creating an echo chamber. The largest chemtrails group on Facebook has over 192,000 members as of January 2021.

Talking with our ex-believers, we learned that *the way in is often the way out*. People who stopped believing in chemtrails often watched a YouTube video they initially thought was pro-chemtrails but was actually anti. Similarly, they joined a Facebook group that they thought was pro-chemtrails but is actually made up of people trying to persuade others not to believe. The media that persuaded people to believe also persuaded some not to believe.

The impact of YouTube on belief in crazy things is so pronounced that in February 2019 the company made a change to its recommendation algorithm: conspiracy videos would no longer be recommended (Rosenblatt 2019). They are still hosted on the platform, but won't show up automatically any more as the next video you might want to watch. Similarly, in March 2019, Facebook announced that posts from anti-vaccination groups would no longer be recommended in people's newsfeeds (Becker 2019). How these companies decide which videos and groups count as being about conspiracies is a critical detail that they have not shared.

The change had a profound impact, and quarterly earnings of YouTube's parent company, Alphabet, declined significantly as a result (Kovach 2019). YouTube was making tremendous profits from convincing people of crazy things. This suggests that a purely capitalistic approach to management of internet companies is no longer sufficient – we can't assume the right thing will magically happen if every company simply works to maximize shareholder value (more about this in Chapter 7). The Association for Computing Machinery (ACM) is the largest professional society in the world for computing professionals. The ACM rewrote its code of ethics in 2018 for the first time in twenty-five years (Gotterbarn et al. 2018). One addition to the code is "3.7 Recognize and take special care of systems that become integrated into the infra-structure of society." It's increasingly apparent that large social media companies have been so integrated, and new regula-tions of their practices are needed, lest they profit from con-vincing people that the earth is flat. Taking a longer view, more attention to the social impact of social media will help those companies to thrive. Working from a profit motive works at least a bit better if we work for a long-term profit. Prioritizing just this quarter's earnings report is toxic. YouTube and Facebook have taken small steps toward doing the right thing, and this will benefit them in the longer term. To really address these problems we will need both more regulation of commercial platforms and support for more non-profit platforms that are motivated by the public good.

## Enter the Trolls

So far we've seen that people working together to contribute and refine information can create knowledge (true, justified information). However, well-meaning people can come to agree on false ideas if they start with incorrect, shared assumptions. They can't correct one another if they all agree on those false assumptions. This is what happens in the case of belief in false conspiracy theories. However, believers in conspiracy theories are typically well-meaning. They sin-cerely believe they are building real knowledge, and that what they are doing is important.

People who participate in flat earth discussions online are a mix of sincere enthusiasts, the occasional profit-eer making money from selling literature and related items (as Rowbotham made money off his lectures), and a subgroup of people who find this entire thing *hilarious* and enjoy egging on sincere participants. The presence of people who are not well-meaning – who are deliberately trying to undermine the knowledge-building process – is another threat to knowledge building. These people are often called "trolls."

In her book *This Is Why We Can't Have Nice Things, Mapping the Relationship between Trolling and Mainstream Culture*, Whitney Phillips asks a troll to define trolling. The troll's answer is: "A troll is a person who likes to disrupt stupid conversations on the Internet. They have two basic rules: nothing should be taken seriously, and if it exists, there is porn of it" (Phillips 2015, 1). Gabriella Coleman elaborates that

> Trolls try to upset people by spreading grisly or disturbing content, igniting arguments, or engendering general bedlam. The chaos of feuding and flaming can be catalyzed by inhabiting identities, beliefs, and values solely for their mischievous potential; by invading online forums with spam; or by ordering hundreds of pizzas, taxis, and even SWAT teams to a target's residence. Whatever the technique, trolls like to say they do what they do for the lulz – a spirited but often malevolent brand of humor etymologically derived from lol. (Coleman 2014, 4)

It's a whole lot harder for collaborative knowledge building to succeed when some people are deliberately trying to mess it up.

Trolls enjoy disrupting online knowledge building. Shachaf and Hara studied trolls on Wikipedia. They observed contributors who repeatedly vandalized content in provocative ways, such as adding pornography. Managing these attacks creates large amounts of work for administrators (Shachaf and Hara 2010). When trolls disrupt forum conversations, it can make it challenging for regular users to participate. Journalist Josh Quittner documented an early example, when the USENET group alt.tasteless decided to attack the group rec.pets.cats. Some of the disruptive posts were direct (like accounts of violent mutilation of cats) and others were more subtle (like posts advocating declawing cats, using language designed to stir up cat lovers who feel strongly on this issue) (Quittner 1994). Nothing is sacred. Following the death of a SeaWorld trainer in front of a live audience in 2010, trolls used her image in a series of dehumanizing and sexualized memes. Whitney Phillips cites this incident as key in a series of events that led to the practice of "RIP trolling," the practice of vandalizing memorial pages for the dead (Phillips 2015).

Trying to counter trolls is an arms race. When site maintainers find ways to undo damage by vandals, the vandals find innovative ways to attack. The cycle is never-ending. Online sites use a mix of human labor and automated means (often called "bots") to remove bad content. Stuart Geiger and David Ribes explain the interaction between humans and bots used to stop vandalism on Wikipedia as an example of distributed cognition (Geiger and Ribes 2010). Software tools help to detect obvious vandalism (like use of swear words, or addition or deletion of large amounts of text), and provide human editors with an easy (one- or two-click) way to undo them and document the offense. The tools greatly reduce the human labor required, and also serve as a connection among groups of editors so they can collaborate effectively.

Wikipedia uses a set of vandal-fighting bots written by volunteers that typically use relatively simple heuristics (rules of thumb) for detection, and automate repetitive actions. Reddit similarly has bots that operate by simple rules, especially the tool "Automod," created by Chad Birch, which uses regular expression matching and lists of explicitly allowed or banned sites for links (Jhaver et al. 2019). These sites are transparent about how their systems work, and rely primarily on the work of volunteers. Large commercial sites like Facebook and Twitter more often rely on a combination of paid workers and more sophisticated artificial intelligence technology like deep learning (Buni and Chemaly 2016; Roberts 2017). None of these sites, however, can afford to be fully transparent about how automated systems work, because that could be exploited to get around the rules – for example, by deliberately misspelling banned terms. For instance, when Instagram banned certain hashtags used for people promoting eating disorders and self-harm, users simply changed the spelling (Chancellor et al. 2016).

Fundamental to the design of systems to promote knowledge building is the idea of peer review. The more people look at something and check it, the more we can be sure it is reliable. From Wikipedia we have learned that, surprisingly, those people don't necessarily have to be experts. People without specialized knowledge can help this process if they follow basic rules of supporting assertions with strong references, and understand what makes a source a good one to rely on. When we add trolls to this picture, things get much more complicated. Now we have an ecosystem of actors, and some are trying to improve the content but others are deliberately undermining the entire process. Techniques used by trolls and vandal-fighters are forever coevolving. I'll return to the topic of managing bad behavior and bad content in Chapter 6.

## Quality of the Product

Content produced by knowledge-building discourse isn't just "the same stuff made a different way." It has intriguingly different qualities. We saw in Chapter 3 that compared to articles written by professional historians, Wikipedia biographies of historical figures are equally accurate, but have more colorful details and less historical interpretation (since that's not allowed) (Rosenzweig 2006). One of the most intriguing differences is in selection of content. When all the people contributing to knowledge-building discourse are volunteers, you naturally get content that is of interest to those volunteers. Returning to our example of the website Company Command, that site naturally supports the growth of content of interest to Company Commanders.

Tailoring content to what members are interested in is mostly a good thing. However, it does sometimes mean that "fun" topics get more attention than more important ones. For example, the Wikipedia article about fantasy author Terry Pratchett has over 15,000 words (as of June 2020, including references), while the article about epistemology has 13,000. Designers of online sites that support knowledge-building discourse can add features to try to encourage the kind of content they hope to see. On Wikipedia, WikiProjects play this role. For example, WikiProject Medicine encourages thoughtful medical articles, and WikiProject Sharks encourages good coverage of sharks.

The exact dynamic of what kind of content volunteers choose to produce varies by platform. How the creator of a platform can encourage some kinds of content and discourage others is a core design challenge for online communities.

## Theoretical Summary

In *knowledge-building discourse*, a group of people all contribute ideas and improve contributions by others. As the success of Wikipedia demonstrates, this can be surprisingly effective.

Knowledge building takes place in *communities of practice*. People learn to become part of a community of practice through a process of *legitimate peripheral participation* (LPP). In LPP, individuals start off contributing to the community in simple ways, observing the contributions of more experienced members, and increasing the sophistication of their contributions over time. While it's easy to observe mature practice in physical labor, such as learning to be a tailor, it's harder to see what a more experienced person is doing in knowledge work. The process of learning via LPP for knowledge work is called *cognitive apprenticeship*. A key to successful cognitive apprenticeship is making others' work visible.

Knowledge building is supported by socio-technical systems – combinations of people, social practices, and tools. The design of the tools used can very much shape the group's activity and the outcome. A *distributed cognition* (dcog) approach suggests that we look at the "thing that is thinking" as a combination of elements of the environment as well as the people and their activities.

While people working together can generate a surprising amount of knowledge, the process can fail if a group starts with wrong assumptions. This is what happens in the case of belief in false conspiracy theories. If a group shares the same false assumptions, then they may fail to critique one another's mistakes. Knowledge building is even more vulnerable when some contributors (vandals and trolls) are deliberately trying to undermine the process.

## Practical Implications

We increasingly rely on knowledge building for a host of important societal functions. We learn things from Wikipedia, and enrich our understanding in discussions on both casual and serious topics. In fact, the entire internet can be viewed as a knowledge-building system. Understanding how knowledge building works, its potential, and its limits, is a skill increasingly necessary for everyday life.

Figuring out how to improve knowledge building and protect against threats to its quality is a key challenge for internet companies and researchers. If a group building knowledge has agreed upon assumptions, it's important to

116

articulate those assumptions explicitly. Then, current members of the group can critique those assumptions and improve them, and potential new members can decide if this group is a good choice for them. Understanding the nature of knowledge building, we can design software to better support it.

# 5 How Do People Express Identity Online, and Why Is This Important for Online Interaction?

W ho are we when we go online, and how do we express that to others? Much internet activity consists of presenting oneself before others in one fashion or another. As a result, how we describe ourselves online shapes online interaction in critical ways. It is one of the most fundamental design choices that we make in creating online sites. To start exploring these issues, we need a nuanced understanding of face-to-face interaction. Erving Goffman's classic 1959 book, *The Presentation of Self in Everyday Life*, is a good place to start. Goffman wrote, "When the individual presents himself before others, his performance will tend to incorporate and exemplify the officially accredited values of the society, more so, in fact, than does his behavior as a whole ... The world, in truth, is a wedding" (Goffman 1959, 35–36).

## The Presentation of Self in Everyday Life

What really is a wedding? At a wedding, everyone dresses up and collectively enacts a ritual that is meant to convey information to the entire group – these two people are now a family. Everyone at the wedding is playing a role – like bride/groom, mother of the bride/groom, the bride/groom's school friends, the officiant, etc. Each participant is supposed to dress and behave in a certain way. We learn these social norms from personal and cultural examples.

I was more nervous before my own wedding than before giving significant professional talks to large audiences. The role of "professor" is one I'm comfortable with. The role of "bride" was unfamiliar. We are all always playing a role, and we play different roles on a daily basis. On a typical day I might drive my teenage son to school, stop off at the allergist for my allergy shot, buy a cup of tea at a café, meet with a graduate student, teach a class, and have a conference call with a collaborator. In each of these situations, I present different sides of who I am. Amy the mom, Amy the allergy sufferer, Amy the tea drinker, Amy the advisor, Amy the teacher, and Amy the research collaborator are all a bit different. I present myself differently in each of these settings. If I swapped two of those performances – for example, if rather than approaching the café counter and addressing the next available staff member to order tea, instead I stood at the front of the café facing everyone and projecting my voice to get everyone's attention as I would at the start of class – the results would be comic and awkward. My behavior in each setting is different, and who I am in each setting is also different. Together, all these aspects make up who I am.

Students in my "Design of Online Communities" class sometimes fall into the trap of thinking of these different facets of ourselves as facades masking our "true selves." In fact, there is no "one true self." It doesn't exist. We are all always performing, and who we are at the core is a synthesis of all these aspects (Turkle 1995, 261).

Goffman has a wealth of insights into human interaction and presentation of the self. It's worth going through
these in detail, because most or all of these have analogs in
online interaction. The original Goffman text is worth reading, though I need to warn you, as I always warn my class,
that it has sections that are offensive (sexist, racist, classist,
etc.) to a more modern sensibility.

Goffman begins simply enough by saying that
"When an individual enters the presence of others, they
commonly seek to acquire information about him or to bring
into play information about him already possessed ...
Information about the individual helps to define the situation,
enabling others to know in advance what he will expect of
them and what they may expect of him" (Goffman 1959, 1).

The most basic thing we need to know in many
situations is someone's official role. To get my allergy shot,
I need to know who (of the dozen people present at the
allergist's office) is the nurse giving shots today. I arrive at
the office and sign in, and the nurse calls my name when
they are ready. I can infer that the person who calls my name
from the room for allergy shots is the shot nurse for today.
Their location (the shot room) and their behavior (calling
my name after I've signed in) convey that information. But if
I am confused, I can support my conclusion by their
clothing – nurses at the office wear medical scrubs and a
badge with their name.

Have you ever confused someone's role? It has
happened to me many times, especially in clothing stores.
I might ask, "Do you know if this comes in other colors?"
and my embarrassed interlocutor replies, "I'm sorry, I don't

work here." I've also been mistaken for the employee. For example, at a recent trip to a clothing store, after I picked a sweater in my size from a pile, I then straightened the pile. A fellow customer saw me straightening clothing, and reasonably assumed that I worked there. These kinds of mistaken interactions can be uncomfortable because, as Goffman notes, having a particular role entitles a person to be treated in a particular way. Mistaken interactions happen often in clothing stores because staff typically do not wear a special uniform, so, unlike with the nurse at the allergist, we are missing attire as a cue to a person's role.

According to Goffman, information we might want to know about someone includes their socio-economic status, their conception of themselves, their attitude toward you, their competence, and their trustworthiness. Goffman assumes we can easily infer someone's gender, age, and race because we can see them. Online, we may (or may not) want ways to infer those aspects of personal identity.

Carriers of that information about the individual in face-to-face settings include clues from a person's behavior and appearance. This includes physical characteristics, how they dress, and how they hold themselves. We also infer information from a person's likelihood of being in a setting – the person calling my name from the shot room is probably the shot nurse, and the person standing at the front of the room at the start of class is probably the teacher.

In face-to-face settings, we are always calculating: What role does everyone here have? Who am I speaking to? As we will see, how we represent identity online shapes how these processes unfold in online interaction.

## Expressions Given and Expressions Given Off

In each setting, we are always consciously and/or unconsciously trying to convey an impression to others. However, how people actually interpret our performance may be different from what we intend. In Goffman's terms, there are *impressions given* (what we intend to convey) and *impressions given off* (what we unintentionally convey) (Goffman 1959, 2). Suppose a host cooks dinner for a visitor, and asks how the food is. The visitor might reply "delicious!" – intending to be graciously appreciative. However, the host might "take note the rapidity with which the visitor lifted his fork or spoon to his mouth, using these signs to check the stated feelings of the eater" (Goffman 1959, 7). The chef is checking impressions given off to try to develop a deeper insight than the guest's polite response. Goffman notes that because we know that people try to control what impression they are making, as interpreters of others' behavior we divide someone's performance into more and less easily controlled aspects. The dinner guest's speech is more easily controlled than the enthusiasm with which they move their fork.

Goffman's story of a guest approaching a Shetland cottage conveys an intriguing interplay between a performer trying to convey a particular image and a recipient interpreting that performance:

> When a neighbor dropped by to have a cup of tea, he would ordinarily wear at least a hint of an expectant warm smile as he passed through the door in the cottage. Since lack of physical obstructions outside the cottage

and lack of light within usually made it possible to observe the visitor unobserved as he approached the house, islanders sometimes took pleasure in watching the visitor drop whatever expression he was manifesting and replace it with a sociable one just before reaching the door. However, some visitors, in appreciating that this examination was occurring, would blindly adopt a social face a long distance from the house, thus ensuring the projection of a constant image. (Goffman 1959, 8)

Here we have a kind of arms race between the visitor trying to convey a particular impression (impressions given) and what the host actually infers (impressions given off).

People's performances can be sincere or cynical. I can try to convey to you that I am an excellent financial advisor because I actually am skilled in that field (sincere) or because I am actually a swindler and would like to convince you to trust me so I can take your money (cynical). To add another layer of complexity, in the case of the sincere performance, I may be correct that I am a skilled advisor or I may be deluded. My interlocuter uses cues to interpret both the sincerity of my performance and my likely actual competence.

Human interaction is fundamentally collaborative. The start of an interaction establishes important expectations on the part of participants. Goffman shares the example of a teacher's approach to the first day of class:

The first day I get a new class in, I let them know who's boss ... You've got to start off tough, and then you can ease up as you go along. If you start off easy-going, when you try to get tough, they'll just look at you and laugh. (Becker 1952, 459; cited in Goffman 1959, 12)

Based on those initial expectations, participants establish a *working consensus* that helps get them through the situation. Once we have established that I am the patient and you are the allergy shot nurse, then we have a set of routines or "scripts" that we follow that help us get through the rest of the interaction smoothly (Schank and Abelson 2013).

## Fronts and Roles

Goffman defines a "front" as "that part of the individual's performance which regularly functions in a general and fixed fashion to define the situation for those who observe the performance" (Goffman 1959, 2). He writes, "as part of personal front we may include: insignias of office or rank; clothing; sex, age, and racial characteristics; size and looks; posture; speech patterns; facial expressions; bodily gestures; and the like" (Goffman 1959, 24). Goffman divides these into appearance and manner (attitudes toward the current situation). We expect appearance and manner to be consistent, and to be consistent with the situation. Different roles may use some of the same elements as part of their front. In Goffman's example, both chimney sweeps and perfume clerks of his time wore white lab coats.

In addition to appearance and manner, the third main element of the front is the setting, "furniture, décor, physical layout, and other background items which supply the scenery and stage props" (Goffman 1959, 22) for human activity that takes place there. Architecture and interior design create contexts that set the tone for human activity.

In some cases, there is a gap between the front and the person's actual role. For example, "A patient will see his nurse stop at the next bed and chat for a moment or two with the patient there. He doesn't know that she is observing the shallowness of his breathing and color and tone of his skin. He thinks she is just visiting" (Goffman 1959, 31). As a result, nurses sometimes don't get the respect they deserve as skilled professionals. Similarly, much of the work of an undertaker is not visible to the customer, the bereaved family. Consequently, undertakers charge a great deal of money for the casket (something the family can see), and this helps cover the cost of all their services (Goffman 1959, 32).

## Identity Online: Usernames

Whether you are playing an official role in an online interaction or just hanging out, you have a personal front. People adapt how they interact with you based on how you present yourself – the elements of your personal front that you use.

At the simplest level, many online sites have textual usernames. In some cases, your username is chosen for you. Everyone at my son's school has to use the username that is their last name, a period, and then their first name, so I am Bruckman.Amy. Standardizing usernames makes it easy to find anyone, and many information technology departments enforce this at schools and corporations.

In the 1990s through early 2000s, some sites for kids like Cartoonnetwork.com standardized usernames by letting you pick from a fixed list of adjectives and nouns

SHOULD YOU BELIEVE WIKIPEDIA?

and adding a number – so you'd end up being something like BraveParrot331. The intent was to give people some degree of choice while making absolutely sure there would be no bad words included, and without having to pay a customer service representative to manage usernames. However, this style of username didn't work particularly well because the restricted choice didn't make you feel like this "was you."

In most cases on the internet, people get to choose their username, and you can tell a surprising amount about a person based on what name they select. Consider the following three usernames from the College of Computing at Georgia Tech:

jalisa
jkh
wedge

To protect people's privacy, I've chosen usernames from people no longer at Georgia Tech, but they were once active names. One of them is a professor, one is an undergraduate, and one is an administrative staff member. Can you guess who is who?

When I do this exercise in class, students almost always get it right. As you might guess, "wedge" is the undergraduate. Later in his career at Georgia Tech, when he became a master's student, he regretted the silly name and begged our technology services organization to change it to his first initial and last name. At the time it was against policy to allow username changes, but someone took pity on wedge and updated it. His sensibilities changed from the time he was a seventeen-year-old freshman to the time he was a master's student trying to build a professional image.

User "jalisa" was an administrative staff member who conveyed a warm and friendly, informal tone by using her first name. User "jkh" was faculty, and used initials for a more professional self-presentation. How we choose to present ourselves online conveys how we see ourselves, and how we feel about the particular online setting.

One question that comes up for administrators is whether to allow obscene usernames. The answer depends on what kind of site you are running. On the bulletin board system ECHO (a kind of New York version of The WELL), founder Stacy Horn decided that she would "let people have whatever id they want. Go ahead, call yourself bigdick. See if I care. I think people would rather know than not know that you are the kind of person who would call themselves bigdick. It says something about you" (Horn 1998, 18). In Stacy's view, someone choosing a rude username is performing a public service by warning everyone what kind of person they are. Allowing rude usernames was a great strategy for ECHO, but wouldn't be appropriate for another site like, for example, one aimed at kids or affiliated with a brand.

Many sites require each username to be unique. Enough of the namespace is taken on large sites like Reddit that it can be hard to find a username that expresses what you want, unless you add a number to the end.

For email, the site hosting your account also conveys information about who you are. Posting from a university or corporate account conveys an official capacity.

In the 1990s, people with university accounts often looked down on people posting from large commercial providers like America Online (Donath 2002). This is less true today, as free email services like Google's Gmail have become widely accepted.

## Elements of Online Identity

Usernames are just one of myriad elements of personal identity we express on online sites. A host of design features contribute to people's online self-presentation. Elements of personal identity that often appear in the official part of an online profile include:

- gender
- topic-specific information (like a model motorcycle on a motorcycle forum, or a diagnosis on a medical forum)
- real name
- a profile picture/image (perhaps a photo, or an image the person chooses)
- a 3D avatar
- the person's past posting history on the site
- links to the person's presence on other sites
- profile text written by the person
- a "character class" the user has chosen (for games)
- membership in subgroups of the site (like guilds, for multiplayer games)
- achievements within the community (like Reddit karma)

Sites like dating sites may delve much deeper into personal information, with details like religion, political orientation, sexual orientation, race, and age. On non-dating sites, race and age are rarely explicitly marked.

When a designer chooses which elements of personal identity are easy to express on a site, the designer is essentially *engineering a new personal front*. Imagine you were starting a face-to-face business, like installing solar panels. Decisions you might make include: Do your employees wear a uniform? If there is no explicit uniform, do you give them guidelines on what to wear? Do they have business cards? Clipboards? Do they drive a car with a company logo? All these decisions affect the impression your employees make on customers – you are designing their front. Similarly, when you are creating a new online site, you decide how users may present themselves to one another – should we have profile pictures? Should users be pseudonymous or identified by real names that we verify? Should we have people state their gender? Which elements you emphasize shapes the kinds of interactions that ensue.

## Gender Online

In 1983, Lindsy Van Gelder was on CompuServe, an early bulletin board system (BBS), and became friends with another user, Joan. Van Gelder tells Joan's story in her 1985 *Ms. Magazine* article, "The Strange Case of the Electronic Lover" (Van Gelder 1985). Joan was a neuropsychologist who had been severely injured in a car accident involving a drunk driver, and had ongoing challenges with both her mobility and speech. Talking on the BBS was her main social outlet. Online, Joan was outgoing, charming, and generous with her time and money. She was also sexually aggressive. She identified as bisexual and was relentless in asking women on the board to have text-based sexual exchanges with her.

Joan introduced a friend on the BBS, Jane, to her friend Alex, a psychiatrist living in Manhattan. Jane and Alex hit it off, and Alex paid to fly Jane to visit him for a lavish weekend. They began a relationship.

By now you may have guessed the punchline to the story – "Joan" was really Alex. Alex had started the "Joan" account out of professional interest in what it felt like to be a woman, but then the experiment spiraled out of control and became something more elaborate and ultimately sinister.

Van Gelder's story is timeless and raises a host of fascinating questions. First, she wonders "why a man has to put on electronic drag to experience intimacy, trust, and sharing" (Van Gelder 1985). Alex genuinely felt that people treated him differently when he was Joan. In what ways does gender shape how you treat people, online and in person? It's well documented that accounts that present as female online often receive unwelcome romantic attention, ranging from flirting to harassment. Is there a degree of "intimacy, trust, and sharing" among women that men don't experience? Alex's experiment gives us a unique way to ask those questions and reflect.

Van Gelder writes that interaction online is "dizzyingly egalitarian, since the most important thing about oneself isn't age, appearance, career success, health, race, gender, sexual preference, accent, or any of the other categories by which we normally judge each other, but one's mind" (Van Gelder 1985). It's a beautiful vision, but to what degree is it true?

My observation is that for text-based communication, we still judge one another – but by a different set of markers. Notably, in writing, one judges by writing skill. Writing skill is a proxy for level of education and privilege. In more visual modes of communication, such as Snapchat and Instagram, traditional identity markers like age and race are back in the forefront of interaction.

Stacy Horn has a different view from Van Gelder. When Horn encounters people online who are gender-swapping, she feels that "You can't always tell. At first. But you can often tell over time. The illusion of free and unbiased communication can only be maintained and then only briefly, as long as people hide. It's a trick. In time, if you act like yourself, gender is revealed, because we do take our bodies with us. I don't log on and suddenly forget I'm female. Oh, I'm online! Now I can forget a lifetime of socialization" (Horn 1998, 85). André Brock agrees, writing that "the digital is the mediator of embodiment and identity, not an escape from it" (Brock 2020, 20).

Questions about how one's real-life gender shapes behavior patterns online became particularly challenging for Horn when she faced a dilemma: whether to let ECHO member "Embraceable Ewe" (who was in the process of transitioning from male to female) into the women-only forum on ECHO, WIT. Horn writes, "I'm in over my head … Is gender a biological or social construct? … If I let her into WIT, will it feel like there is a man in the room, or a woman?" (Horn 1998, 82). When Horn started ECHO, she didn't anticipate having to be the arbiter of questions like the fundamental nature of gender!

To answer the question of whether to invite a transitioning person into an all-female group, we need to have a more nuanced understanding of why we are creating a single-gender space in the first place. Oldenburg notes that the Third Place (see Chapter 1) is often single-gender (Oldenburg 1989). What are we trying to achieve with explicitly single-gender online spaces? Today, many spaces self-select as predominantly one gender, but few have explicit gender restrictions. Ultimately, Horn allowed Embraceable to join WIT after she met a series of criteria, but writes that she regrets not simply accepting Embraceable as who she says she is. Our sensibilities on this topic have evolved since the 1990s.

Who is right, Van Gelder or Horn? Is the online world "dizzily egalitarian" or can you "always tell"? To explore this question, then-Georgia Tech graduate student Joshua Berman and I created a multiplayer identity game called The Turing Game, which we launched in 1999 (Berman and Bruckman 2001). The Turing Test is a challenge to see how far artificial intelligence has progressed – can a person tell the difference between written answers to questions from a person and a computer? In Alan Turing's original paper about the Turing Test, he explains it first in terms of a gender test. Imagine that you have a man in one room and a woman in the other, and you can only communicate with them by slipping typed questions under the door. Could you tell who is who based on how they answer? Turing goes on to ask the reader to now imagine that there is a human behind one door and a computer behind the other. However, Berman and I returned to his first example about gender.

In The Turing Game, a panel of volunteers all pretend to be a particular identity. Any identity is possible, and game types were chosen by users. Suppose everyone is pretending to be women. The panelists are supposed to answer questions as if they are women, and each chooses a woman's name as a temporary pseudonym. Some really are women, and some are not. The audience votes to say who they believe. A moderator chooses among questions suggested by the audience. When the moderator decides the game is over, everyone's real identity is revealed and a discussion ensues about how the audience knew the truth or how they were fooled. Here's an example from a game where people were pretending to be women:

QUESTION: Describe your last really bad haircut.

PENNY: I had it layered and I got a perm. Since my hair is wavy, it was Annie style.

WENDY: Sophomore year, decided to cut it really short, and I looked like a little boy. My boyfriend was very disturbed.

Most people correctly guess that "Penny" is really a woman and "Wendy" is not. The reasons are interesting to reflect on. At the simplest level, the real woman shows a deeper knowledge of women's hairstyles. But more interestingly, the person pretending to be a woman is worried about what her boyfriend thinks rather than what she herself thinks. In my experience, women tend to worry more about what they themselves think.

The game quickly became popular, with 12,000 users from all seven continents over the course of a year. People played with all different sorts of identity categories in addition to gender – like guessing who is really over 30, or who is Canadian. It was particularly popular with people who were transitioning their gender, people under house arrest, and the staff at a research station in Antarctica (there's not much to do there over the long, dark winter!). The point of the game was to get people discussing these issues of identity, and to develop some deeper insights into how people act online and how your personal identity shapes those interactions. And it did – sort of.

Analyzing data from games played, we found that people often made decisions based on stereotypes. For example, someone might say "I knew player two was a woman because she used such long sentences." This is grounded in the idea that women use long, flowery sentences with lots of dependent clauses and men say things like "I'll be back." The only problem is that this idea is just a stereotype. Studies of how many words men and women use per turn have different answers depending on whether they're talking to men or women, the medium of conversation, etc. A blanket "women talk more" stereotype is false (Baron 2004; Fox et al. 2007). The game surfaced stereotypes (some false, some true), and reinforced them, but didn't help people to distinguish stereotype from reality.

The second problem with The Turing Game as an interactive, philosophical experience is that the first thing you really want to know before judging someone's performance is how many times they have played the game. For example, in one game in which people were pretending to be women, one question was: "What's your favorite alcoholic drink?" One respondent said, "scotch on the rocks." The audience correctly reasoned that a man pretending to be a woman wouldn't say that, and that was true in that particular case. But now that you know that trick, you might consider trying a double reversal to fool people (like the movie *Victor Victoria*).

The ultimate lesson from The Turing Game is that we need to work hard to distinguish between stereotypes and empirically verifiable reality. And those are moving targets – both the stereotypes and the reality are always evolving.

In the end, Van Gelder and Horn are both partially right. Sometimes this new mode of interaction can be surprisingly egalitarian, and sometimes not. The exact details of how sites are designed and how people can present themselves matter.

## Identity Workshop

"Joan" was playing with aspects of identity online. Online, you can pretend to be someone you're not, and that process can help you reflect on your face-to-face identity and sense of self. The internet can be a kind of "identity workshop." That was the title of my final paper in Sherry Turkle's class on sociology of technology in 1992. Taking Turkle's class and serving as her research assistant for part of her book *Life on the Screen* (Turkle 1995) were transformative experiences in my graduate-school career.

SHOULD YOU BELIEVE WIKIPEDIA?

Turkle thinks deeply about the psychological foundations of our interactions with computers. In her 1984 book, *The Second Self, Computers and the Human Spirit*, she wrote about Deborah, a young girl who was concerned about issues of control in her life. When Deborah learned to program a computer in Logo, she was engaging in an intellectual exploration of issues of control, a key emotional and psychological issue she was struggling with at the time (Turkle 1984). Most research on humans and computers stays relatively at the surface: this is what people like, this is what people do. Turkle pushes deeper to understand *why* people like certain activities, and why they engage in them. And the answers to those questions are not superficial – they are about who we are and who we wish to become in the most profound sense.

My class paper explored concepts of identity in MUDs, text-based virtual-reality environments that were popular at the time (see Chapter 1). A MUD is like any massively multiplayer game, except that the whole world is created in text (for example, the description of The Living Room on a MUD called LambdaMOO begins: "It is very bright, open, and airy here, with large plate-glass windows looking southward over the pool to the gardens beyond . . ."). In addition to describing objects and places, you can describe yourself. Because you can easily describe yourself as anything you want, it becomes easy to experiment with identity. The following summer, I helped Turkle study MUDs further, assisting with research for *Life on the Screen* (Turkle 1995).

Turkle is a psychoanalyst, and one fundamental question she asked about this online identity play was:

Does it help? If people are playing with concepts of identity, are they growing in a healthy way as a result? We wrestled with this basic question all summer, and had no conclusion by September when I went back to my regular research at the Media Lab. Her final conclusion in the book is: sometimes. For some of the people we interviewed, they explored personal issues they were struggling with for a period of time, and later made life changes that showed growth. Others just struggled more and more. In psychological terms, some were "working through" and others were "acting out." The technology is evocative, but a range of things can happen as a result.

## Identity Deception

Gender-swapping is just one form of identity deception that takes places online. People can present themselves differently from their real selves in any dimension of personal identity. In some contexts, your real identity is expected, and deviating from that is breaking a social norm. In others, identity play is welcome and expected.

Understanding deception is one way to develop insights into how identity functions in online social groups more generally. Judith Donath explains deception in terms of ideas borrowed from research on animal behavior: *assessment signals* and *conventional signals* (Donath 2002). An assessment signal is a reliable signal that demonstrates the trait being shown. For example, having big muscles is an assessment signal for strength. Displaying an assessment signal is costly to the sender, because they need to really have that trait. On the other hand, a conventional signal is one that's easy to fake. For example, wearing a "Gold's Gym" T-shirt is a conventional signal for strength.

When we interact online, some signals become easier to fake. It takes quite a bit of work to present as someone of a different gender in a face-to-face setting (with clothing, changed personal manner, etc.), but online it may be as simple as one click.

Donath notes that the world of deceptive and true signals creates an ecosystem. In butterflies, there are monarch butterflies that use their bright coloring to tell birds that they are not tasty to eat. There are also moths that mimic monarchs in appearance. The moths are tasty, but birds avoid them because they look like monarchs. The more moths imitate monarchs, the more a bird might consider eating something that looks like a monarch – the odds of it being tasty go up. Having lots of deceivers brings a cost to the non-deceptive members of the system.

Many online interactions are low-stakes – it may not really matter if the person you are chatting with is not really as they describe themselves (as long as you're not relying on them for medical or legal advice!). One higher-stakes example is dating sites. If someone lies about who they are, people may waste time they could spend talking with someone more suitable, and may have uncomfortable face-to-face encounters. Toma et al. wondered how much people lie on dating sites. To find out, they had people on dating sites come into a lab setting and compared their online profiles to their real selves. They looked at people's driver's licenses to confirm age, measured their height, and had them step on a scale to get an accurate weight. They found that people generally do lie – but just a little bit. If you are hoping to eventually meet someone face-to-face, lying a lot isn't strategic. However, stretching the truth just a bit is so tempting that most people do it. Eight out of ten people lied in at least one category. They write, "weight was the most frequently lied about attribute, followed by height, and least of all age. For those identified as lying on an item, the magnitude of the deception was usually small. The average deception for height was only 2.09% of the participants' actual height, 5.5% of the participants' actual weight, and 1.4% of the participants' actual age" (Toma et al. 2008). The ecosystem of people being more or less truthful on online dating sites is like the ecosystem of butterflies and moths – deceptive presentations create a cost for others.

## Age and Race

Gender is the most studied component of online identity, but is not necessarily the most important. It's an interesting research question in itself to think about why researchers to date have been so focused on gender and have paid less attention to other aspects of identity. Other factors like age arguably shape how you interact with others in face-to-face interactions more.

Age is too often neglected in research. In her master's thesis on online role-playing of Harry Potter fan fiction on LiveJournal, Casey Fiesler found that many people were role-playing erotic scenes, not realizing that their scene partner might be under-age. Acting out a sex scene with a teenager is not only creepy, it's potentially a serious illegal act. It just never occurred to the LiveJournal role-players to check someone's age, especially since the social norm of the group was to not ask people about their real-life identities (Fiesler 2007).

Age is particularly salient as an aspect of identity in countries where age strongly shapes interpersonal interaction. In Korea, the language itself changes depending on how old the person you are addressing is – you use different words to talk to someone older than to talk to a peer. A Korean student in my "Design of Online Communities" class once told me that he believes that the notable popularity of massively multiplayer online games in Korea is linked to that fact. Online, Koreans address everyone as a peer, and he believes that makes online interaction particularly satisfying for them. It would be interesting to try to study whether the student's intuition is correct.

Race is often not expressed in online interaction. André Brock laments that the default internet user is middle class, white, and heterosexual. As we'll see, spaces like Black Twitter help to decenter that whiteness, making a space where Black people "do not feel compelled to hide or change their cultural particularities" (Brock 2020, 87).

## Identity and Communities Focused on a Specific Demographic

The internet was initially developed from the 1960s to early 1980s by largely white, male engineers at research universities. In its formative years, that demographic was dominant.

Personal identity often went unmarked, and if it was unmarked people assumed others they were interacting with were white (or Asian) males – the stereotypes for computer scientists and engineers at the time. As the internet became a mass phenomenon in the 1990s, this changed. During the first dotcom boom in the late 1990s, when early internet companies thrived and venture capital was widely available for any internet idea, a number of niche online sites were created to appeal to other demographics. For example, the site iVillage was launched in 1995 to appeal to women. Around the same time, Third Age was launched to appeal to older adults, and Black Planet to appeal to African-Americans.

In the early days of iVillage, developers tried to create content to appeal to people like themselves – technologically literate, college-educated women. Over time as actual internet users became more diverse, the site was re-focused on the kind of content that you might find in a women's magazine sold in a supermarket checkout line, with articles about topics like weight loss, dating, clothes, and makeup. A similar pattern occurred on many sites. When I interned at Third Age, a website for older adults, in summer 1997, the site was investing lots of money in hiring freelance writers to write thoughtful long-form articles on topics like how your worldview changes when you retire, and how to manage finances on a fixed income. However, looking at the web server logs, they realized that those articles were hardly being read. Instead, users were doing puzzles and using the dating personals. The same lesson again can be seen when Christian Sandvig studied a community network installed on a Native American reservation in 2004. Sandvig documents how tribe members emphasize the educational value of the network when describing it to visitors, but in day-to-day practice their use looks like the use of any other group of people – lots of gaming and online shopping (Sandvig 2012). The lesson here is a deeply human one: people are people. If people in general are interested in a particular kind of content, people in a subgroup will likely have similar interests.

I draw two critical lessons from these cases. First, to build a successful site, it's important to do user-centered design. Online community designers need to gather actual data from potential users before assuming what those people will want. Second, it's important to have online sites that represent a wide range of interests for different people – both ones with makeup tips and ones with essays on the future of intersectional feminism. However, as a site designer, if you are driven solely by maximizing your page views and hence advertising revenue, then you'll get all dating tips and no thoughtful essays. *Being driven solely by the profit motive is breaking the internet.* Yes, to create the highest possible membership on a women's site you need to post stereotypical content. However, it is possible to deliberately choose to promote a different sort of content, if maximizing advertising revenue is not your only concern.

As an example, the website Rookie Magazine (www .rookiemag.com) was created by a fifteen-year-old girl and had articles written by girls and young women on topics like "Meaningful Transformations, my favorite movies about change" and "The Last Train Ride, a story about friendships that fade." It was deliberately non-commercial, and focused on content that matched the founder's values.

Rookie Magazine published issues for seven years, and then folded in 2018 due to business issues. It's interesting to think about whether a site like this could be financially sustainable. One thing, though, is clear: It is impossible if initial funding comes from venture capitalists who demand a high rate of return on their investment.

## Subgroup Conversation in a Public Space: Black Twitter

Most communities that focus on one particular demographic try to create a separate space just for that group. Membership may be explicitly restricted, or expectations of who belongs may lead to self-selection. For example, some Facebook groups for mothers also allow fathers to participate, and others don't.

An intriguing exception to this pattern of membership is Black Twitter (Brock 2012; Manjoo 2019). André Brock writes that "Black Twitter is an online gathering (not quite a community) of Twitter users who identify as Black and employ Twitter features to perform Black discourses, share Black cultural commonplaces, and build social affinities" (Brock 2020, 81). While sites like Reddit divide people into sub-communities and let social norms evolve differently in each subgroup, Twitter is one huge, undivided stream of content. Your main Twitter feed shows content only from people you follow. You can also search for terms or hashtags (#term), and interact with others who post about those topics. Conversations of interest to Black members of Twitter emerge from relevant hashtags, and also from follower relationships.

Black Twitter builds on African-American cultural practices. For example, Sarah Florini discusses the practice of "signifyin'," "a genre of linguistic performance that allows for communication of multiple levels of meaning simultaneously, most frequently involving wordplay and misdirection" (Florini 2014, 224). Florini writes that "Signifyin' serves as an interactional framework that allows Black Twitter users to align themselves with Black oral traditions, to index Black cultural practices, to enact Black subjectivities, and to communicate shared knowledge and experiences" (Florini 2014, 224). Similarly, it builds on oral traditions of call-and-response (Manjoo 2019). Some of the discourse is playful and focused on humor, creating a supportive sense of being in the presence of like-minded others. Black Twitter also has an activist focus, using the platform to draw attention to social issues like police brutality (De Choudhury et al. 2016).

While a site like a subreddit or a Facebook group has a space that is dedicated to that topic and group of members, Twitter conversation is all public. A small fraction of users have private accounts that only approved people can see; however, this is uncommon. As a result, this in-crowd conversation is taking place in view of a diverse audience. This at times is an opportunity for mutual understanding across groups, but also a catalyst for tension among those groups.

## Privacy

We don't always want to reveal everything about ourselves online. Before I discuss online anonymity and pseudonymity, I need to take a detour to introduce basic ideas about privacy. What is privacy and why does it matter?

Privacy is the right to control a "zone of accessibility" around yourself. It includes freedom from intrusion, the ability to control information about oneself, and freedom from surveillance (Baase 2013, 48). Privacy lets us be ourselves, lets us remove our "public persona," and is arguably important for individuality and freedom (Quinn 2017). Simson Garfinkel writes that:

> The problem with the world "privacy" is that it falls short of conveying the really big picture. Privacy isn't just about hiding things. It's about self-possession, autonomy, and integrity. As we move into the computerized world of the twenty-first century, privacy will be one of our most important civil rights. But this right of privacy isn't the right of people to close their doors and pull down their window shades – perhaps because they want to engage in some sort of illicit or illegal activity. It's the right of people to control what details about their lives stay inside their own house and what leaks to outside. (Garfinkel 2000, 4)

I teach about privacy each year in my class "Computing, Society, and Professionalism" (our required undergraduate class on ethics and social implications of technology). Over the years, I've found that the most important concept is the trade-off between *free-market approaches* and *consumer-protection approaches* (Baase 2013, 107–110).

In a *free-market approach*, companies may treat user privacy as they wish. Consumers are encouraged to use voice and exit (see Chapter 6) to respond if they are not satisfied with how a company is treating them. In other words, if you don't like the privacy protections on a site, you can speak up or go to another site.

On the other hand, a *consumer-protection approach* suggests that people are often not able to make well-informed decisions about their privacy. First, they may not even know what data is being collected about them. This is particularly true of "invisible" forms of data collection, like tracking RFID tags or GPS coordinates. Second, most people don't read privacy policies on sites they use. They don't and they couldn't if they tried. The reading level of these policies is well above the level of the average internet user (Jensen and Potts 2004), and reading all the policies for sites you use would simply take too much time (McDonald and Cranor 2008). People are not in a good position to make smart choices about their own privacy.

MIT professor Jerry Saltzer once told me, "privacy is a database correlation problem." What ends up being most invasive is not the data from any single site, but the cross-referencing of data across different sites. Also problematic is the use of data for secondary purposes – uses other than the ones the data was collected for. If people have no reasonable way to envision secondary uses of data, they can't make informed choices about how much data to share.

If people can't make informed choices about how much personal information to share, this argues that we need to pass laws to protect individuals' privacy. However, some argue that the more restrictions we put on how businesses deal with user data, the more we reduce productivity and slow innovation. There are advantages and disadvantages to each approach. It is a trade-off – one that we need to carefully assess in each situation.

## Social Networks and Privacy

My second post when I started my blog in January 2010 is entitled "Amy's Prediction: In 20 Years No One Will Be Qualified to Be President":

> Today's teens are pouring their most personal thoughts onto the Internet. They flirt, they gossip, they angst, they brag about being naughty—just like we did when we were teens. Except the problem is, the Internet is a surprisingly persistent medium.
>
> An old joke says that taking information off the Internet is like taking pee out of a pool. Sure you deleted it, but did the server keep a backup? There's likely a backup on Brewster Kahle's Internet Archive, http://archive.org. Before you decided to delete it, did a friend save a copy? When you post information online, you lose control of it.
>
> Teens say the most amazing things. My friends and I had a great deal of fun, and I'm relieved to say it's all forgotten or at least not documented in my own words or photos. (If I appear doing anything unseemly in my friend Anne Mini's new novel, I can simply deny it!) If all of our coming-of-age angst was saved for posterity, I'd be appalled. I think most people look back on their teen and young adult years that way. At least I hope they do.
>
> What happens when young adult antics are archived? The thought gives one pause. Will the bride data mine the groom before the wedding (or vice versa)? Will the colleague with an axe to grind dig up ancient history to

use as a weapon? Are we entering a new age of
harassment by ancient history, a golden age of blackmail?

I suspect that most teen and young adult antics will
stay obscure, and if they're uncovered folks will mostly
just laugh and reminisce. But there's one special category
of people who may not get away so easy: public figures.
Actors, musicians, and athletes can probably survive the
scrutiny. But what about politicians? We still elected Bill
Clinton, because he said he "didn't inhale." What
happens when the future political candidate is inhaling
on camera, memorialized for posterity?

I see a few possible outcomes. One is that teens over time
will learn to be more careful with their personal
information. This I think is inevitable. Which leads us to
the prospect that we will have one lost generation of
potential future politicians—the generation who didn't yet
know to be careful about their personal information online.
Like the donut hole in Medicare coverage, we'll have a lost
zone between those too old to have been online much and
those young enough to know to be at least a bit careful.

Another potential outcome is that we as a culture will
learn to be more tolerant of what people do in their
personal lives, especially as youth. Europeans tend to be
somewhat more tolerant already—to draw a clearer line
between personal and professional behavior. Americans
are plagued by an endearing notion of "Character"—that
what we do in our personal lives speaks to our fitness for
professional tasks. When complete lives are increasingly
archived, we may need to step back from that ideal and
let our leaders be human. (Bruckman 2010)

Eleven years later, I'd say my prediction is on track. As we
interact online, we continually leak little details about

ourselves. The problem is usually not any one piece of information, but the total picture that comes from the synthesis of those details.

Many years ago in my "Online Communities" class (around 2001), master's student Alisa Bandlow studied people role-playing on the site LiveJournal. Some of the content included erotica. Bandlow asked one of her interview subjects how they felt about the fact that all this content was visible online, linked to their account which used their real name. After the interview, the subject *deleted their account and all their postings*. It hadn't previously crossed their mind to be concerned. Over time, people are becoming more aware that they need to be careful about their online privacy. One way to protect your privacy is to not use your real name for segments of your online activity.

## From Anonymous to Identified

I talked earlier about email account names, and the ways that the account name you choose or are assigned expresses who you are to others. This holds not just for email addresses, but for account names we sign up for on online platforms.

An online username is a "signifier." It's a symbol that points to a person in the real world, the "signified." Semiotics studies the relationship between signifiers and signifieds, and how language makes meaning (de Saussure 1959). A signifier is typically arbitrary. There's nothing about the name "Amy" that is specific to me – it's just a sequence of sounds.

Many online usernames are "identified," which in semiotic terms means there is a publicly visible relationship between the online account (the signifier) and the real-world entity (the person). Other sites can be "anonymous" or "pseudonymous." These are sometimes confused and the distinction is important. On a pseudonymous site, a user has a persistent pseudonym that refers to them. Reddit is an example. For example, "shiruken" is the pseudonym of one of my fellow Reddit moderators. I know that he is male, that he is a biomedical engineer, that he runs our statistics on who had the most mod actions each month, and that he has a variety of scientific interests. I don't actually know his real name or where he lives. In semiotic terms, there is still a relationship here between the signifier and the signified. His Reddit username is not his real name, but it is still a signifier that refers to him, the real person, as the signified.

Pseudonyms operate similarly to "real names." The name I was given at birth is a signifier that has a legal relationship to me, the human. Just like pseudonyms, the relationship between this signifier and the signified can be slippery. I might legally change my name, use a fake name, or be a victim of mistaken identity. For both real names and pseudonyms, there is a signifier with a complicated relationship to the signified. My "real" name has a legal status but otherwise operates in similar ways to pseudonyms I use.

What is a "real name" can be surprisingly controversial. Facebook requires users to use their real name, and users can report another account for violating the real-names policy. Facebook reviews millions of such reports per year. Enforcement of this policy has caused problems for a variety of groups, including people transitioning their gender, drag queens who wish to use a stage name, Native

Americans who wish to use a tribal name, and survivors of domestic abuse, bullying, and stalking.[1] Enforcing a particular legal notion of a real name is a form of oppression in these cases (boyd 2011). In 2015, Facebook introduced explicit support for name changes in those special cases (Facebook 2015), but there continues to be tension around this issue.

"Identified," "pseudonymous," and "anonymous" are not discrete categories, but rather a continuum. As we move from more nearly identified to more nearly anonymous, the relationship between the signifier and the signified gets looser, but it's still there.

When you use a pseudonym over a long period of time, you continually leak little details about yourself (unless you're careful not to). In the course of conversation, you might mention things you like and dislike, places you've been, schools you've attended, and more. The longer you use a pseudonym, the more it de facto identifies the real person. Each leaked detail links the signifier and signified more tightly together.

For this reason, users on Reddit will often create a temporary ("throwaway") account when they really want privacy, often using "throwaway" in the name. If you only use an account for one discussion (usually on a difficult or embarrassing topic), then it is less tied to your real identity than an account that has an accumulation of leaked details about you (Leavitt 2015). Ammari et al. found that Reddit users on parenting boards who used throwaway accounts

---

[1] https://en.wikipedia.org/wiki/Facebook_real-name_policy_controversy

were more likely to discuss stigmatized topics like pregnancy loss, divorce, or custody issues. Posts by throwaway accounts were more likely to get a response, and got more long responses (Ammari et al. 2019).

While a site like Reddit operates with pseudonyms, sites like 4chan are closer to truly anonymous. Posting on 4chan does not require any kind of account or login. Furthermore, most posts disappear within minutes and are not archived (Bernstein et al. 2011). Even if you leak something about what you are interested in with a particular post, it is not linked to all your other posts.

Even at the ends of the spectrum from most nearly identified to most nearly anonymous, there is still a degree of uncertainty. You can imagine that a determined person (e.g., a spy) could falsify an identified account, pretending to be someone they are not. Further, you can imagine that even on an anonymous site, if a government had a compelling need to find someone, government agencies might be able to trace internet traffic to help locate the real person. As a result, it's not a matter of whether we are identified or anonymous – it's more a matter of how hard it is to trace the link from the online presence to the real person. This ranges from easy to very hard.

## Why We Need Pseudonymity

Where to place a site on the continuum from anonymous to identified is a key design decision. Anonymity/pseudonymity is particularly valuable for situations where people may wish to disclose highly personal information – such as in support groups. It's also critical for people who live under oppressive regimes.

While those dramatic cases are important, there are many reasons why ordinary people might want to express themselves pseudonymously on a day-to-day basis. First is the issue of "context collapse" (Vitak 2012). We all present different aspects of who we are in different contexts. For example, you may want to discuss politics on the internet, but not share your political views with your professional colleagues. A functioning democracy requires places to debate issues of the day, but a professional workplace is typically not an appropriate venue for those discussions. Similarly, you might not want to make your interests and hobbies part of a professional persona. The inverse is also true: If you are playing a massively multiplayer video game, you may not want to disclose that you are a professor for your day job! Pseudonymity lets me be both a serious scholar and a fan of the television show *Grey's Anatomy* and to keep those personas separate.

The second issue is permanence. I am eternally grateful that the internet did not exist when I was a teenager – I'm sure I would have said things that mortify me today. Does everything I say need to be part of my permanent record? Judith Donath writes that online

> the product review you generously provided for an underarm deodorant or for books about coping with binge eating or bed-wetting, will, if written under your real name, be part of your online portrait, what your neighbors, kids and random strangers see about you. Online, words persist forever, in vast searchable

databases. Anything you say or do using your real name is permanently attached to it. (Donath 2014)

As a culture, we have not yet quite sorted out how to handle the problem of permanence of information. If someone did something culturally insensitive or racist (like wearing "blackface") decades ago, does that disqualify them for public office now? When is saying "sorry" enough, and when is it not? Because more people are becoming aware of the risks of permanence, sites like Snapchat that make communication ephemeral are becoming more popular. A picture shared on Snapchat goes away in a day, and the system does its best to prevent others from making a copy. (They unfortunately can't stop people from using another camera to photograph the screen.) Snapchat is used by teenagers for hanging out, while a site with permanence like Instagram is used for curating a self-presentation.

## Anonymity and Accountability

Pseudonymity is not always appropriate. In 1995, I started a site called MediaMOO, a professional community for media researchers (Bruckman and Resnick 1995). A MOO is an end-user programmable, text-based virtual world. The MOO software was created by Pavel Curtis, then at Xerox PARC. MediaMOO was kind of like an endless conference reception for a conference on media and human–computer interaction. When I first created the site, I allowed people to have two accounts: one anonymous and one identified by a member's real name. Curtis told me that was silly – why would anyone want to go to a professional conference and hide their name badge or wear a bag over their head? The whole point was to meet other people and network. MediaMOO tried the two-account solution for a few years, but I eventually realized that Curtis was right. I changed our policy to specify that new accounts were to be identified only. Old anonymous ones were allowed to persist, but were rarely used. MediaMOO is an example of a context in which being identified is more appropriate.

Anonymity/pseudonymity also have a major downside: The lack of accountability can lead to bad behavior. The next chapter will talk in detail about bad behavior online and what to do about it.

The image boards 4chan and 8chan are intriguing examples of sites that are more nearly truly anonymous. This has led to a proliferation of content that many people find extremely offensive, including highly explicit images, racism, anti-Semitism, and ideas from the alt-right. The sites often also originate attacks on others, such as "brigading," where individuals encourage large numbers of people to harass individuals on other sites. In 2019, perpetrators of mass shootings posted about their plans on 8chan three separate times. As a result, 8chan's domain name service was shut down, but it remains accessible on the dark web.

It's important to note that 4chan is also a sort of "internet meme factory" which has given us things like "LOLcats," and also held animal abusers accountable (Bernstein et al. 2011). Gabriella Coleman tells in detail the story of how the group "Anonymous" originated on 4chan, and over time parts of the hacker group evolved into a "hacktivist" group trying to work toward social justice (Coleman 2014).

It's possible to be well behaved on an anonymous site, and to create havoc on an identified site. The difference is that an agent of chaos on an identified site is more likely to experience real-world consequences, since the link between their online presence and real identity is stronger. Those consequences serve as a deterrent to bad behavior.

## The Future of Online Identity

The current mechanisms for representing identity online are woefully inadequate. Last week I was followed on Twitter by several fake accounts. I suspected they were fake because their interests had no relationship to mine, and they had few tweets to date. A quick image search showed that they had profile photos stolen from other online sources. Many such accounts are aimed at political manipulation – they create an online history that makes them appear to be a normal person, and then later use the account to spread political propaganda. There should be a way to simply say "that's not a real person – they can't follow me." Similarly, there should be a way to say "that's not a real company – they can't send me email," or "that's a child – they shouldn't be using this site with explicit sexual content." All of these problems – political manipulation of elections, spam, children exposed to explicit content, and more – are fundamentally failures of mechanisms for online identity.

Would it be possible to design a new *identity layer* for the internet? I can make a better decision about whether to talk to a potential new contact if I know whether they really are affiliated with the company or school they claim, whether they really are a friend of one of my friends, etc. If we could tell who is who, we could stop spam, stop deliberate manipulation of our public discourse by foreign operatives, prevent kids from getting to inappropriate content, prevent phishing attacks, and more.

Identity goes hand-in-hand with *reputation*. I imagine a system of *reputation servers*. A reputation server could verify that someone isn't a known bad actor, and estimate their qualifications with regard to a particular topic. Reputation needs to be multi-dimensional – that is, I might have a strong reputation as an expert on human–computer interaction but a weak reputation as a keeper of tropical fish (since I have just a small freshwater tank with easy-to-care-for fish). Further, some aspects of reputation may need to be relative to an individual's position on a particular issue – in other words, Jane has an excellent reputation as a chef for omnivores, but not for vegetarians. There would have to be competing reputation services, so individuals could pick a service they trust. Further, the design of such a system would have to make careful use of cryptography to protect people's privacy.

Unfortunately, it's hard to imagine identity and reputation data that can't be manipulated to mine data about citizens. Further, being identified creates serious risks for members of marginalized groups and people who live under oppressive regimes. How to improve our management of online identity without putting those groups at even more risk may be an impossibly hard design problem. But that doesn't mean our current system is the best that is possible. The challenge is: Can we design improved versions of identity and reputation that help us tell who is who, but in a privacy-preserving way? The potential risks and gains are both high.

## Theoretical Summary

As Erving Goffman described in *The Presentation of Self in Everyday Life* (Goffman 1959), we are all always performing for others. We try to make a particular kind of impression on people we interact with, and we do that differently in each social context. There is no "true self" – we are all a synthesis of different aspects of the self that we present.

To do this, we use "fronts." A front includes both our appearance and manner. An observer divides people's self-presentation into more and less easily controlled aspects, and judges performances more on the less easily controlled. The impression a performer wishes to make is their "impressions given," and the impression the observers actually form are the "impressions given off." Performances may be sincere or cynical.

Online, we similarly are always trying to make an impression. The key difference is that all the elements of our expressive vocabulary are explicitly chosen by site designers.

One critical choice in site design is whether usernames should be more nearly anonymous, pseudonymous, or identified. A name (whether legal real-world name or online account name) is a "signifier" that has a relationship to a "signified." As we move along the spectrum from anonymous to identified, the relationship between the signifier and signified gets stronger. Where a site should be along this continuum depends on the site's purpose.

There are legitimate uses of anonymous communications, notably support groups and communication under oppressive regimes. However, being more nearly anonymous can lead to reduced accountability.

## Practical Implications

Identity is fundamental to the design of social media and the design of the internet. In person, we dress and behave differently in different social situations. Online, the same mechanisms operate. However, online site designers have the power to choose what elements of identity it is possible to express and which are emphasized. These choices profoundly shape online interaction.

# 6    What Is Bad Online Behavior, and What Can We Do About It?

Julian Dibbell begins his article "A Rape in Cyberspace":

> They say he raped them that night. They say he did it
> with a cunning little doll, fashioned in their image and
> imbued with the power to make them do whatever he
> desired. They say that by manipulating the doll he
> forced them to have sex with him, and with each other,
> and to do horrible, brutal things to their own bodies.
> And though I wasn't there that night, I think I can
> assure you that what they say is true, because it all
> happened right in the living room – right there amid the
> well-stocked bookcases and the sofas and the fireplace –
> of a house I came later to think of as my second home.
> (Dibbell 1993, 36)

The incident in question took place in the early 1990s on LambdaMOO, a text-based virtual world (or "MUD," multi-user dungeon) created at Xerox PARC by Pavel Curtis. Interaction on LambdaMOO is all in text. The game can print things like "Pavel looks around the room," or "Pavel pats you on the head." Except the perpetrator in this incident, who went by the username Mr. Bungle, made it look like the people were doing violent, sexual things to themselves.

Although the title of the article refers to "rape," calling a text message a "rape" is inappropriate, because it undermines the seriousness of real rape. Regardless of what you call the incident, the recipients found the messages highly unwelcome. It was a form of online harassment.

In the wake of this incident, the volunteer administrators of the site ("wizards") had a problem: There was nothing in the code of rules for the site that clearly prohibited this behavior. While most community members advocated banning the offender, some people felt that it was wrong to ban someone since there was no rule against it. More provocatively, some argued that it's "just a game," and the recipient of those messages could have blocked the offender or simply logged off. This raises a fundamental question: Is this virtual world a place with expectations of civil behavior, or is it a playground to blow off steam and do things you can't do in the real world? The debate about what to do in response quickly became philosophical.

One wizard did decide to ban Mr. Bungle, and then an uproar ensued – did he have the authority to do that? In response to the controversy, Curtis declared that the wizards would no longer make social policy. This created a governance vacuum where nothing could be decided. Curtis was hoping to separate technical and social decision-making, but quickly learned they were inextricable. A few years later, he created a direct democracy where users could vote on issues facing the community with a system of petitions and ballots. Anyone can write a petition, and if it gets enough signatures, then it becomes a ballot which the community votes on.

In the end, it turned out that the LambdaMOO character that committed the offense was controlled not by one person but by a group of college students. The students were taking turns controlling the keyboard and egging one another on, each trying to be even more outrageous. This detail has always struck me as profound. Humans in groups can behave in much more extreme ways than they ever would individually.

There are a lot of Mr. Bungles on the internet today – more and more over time it seems. What should we do about it? This challenge has three key parts. First, how do we decide what sort of behavior is allowed for a particular site? Social norms are not universal. Each subgroup has to determine what sort of conduct is allowed in their space. A key feature of the internet is that we can have different spaces for radically different sorts of content. Second, how do we help people to know what the social norms for a site are? It's not just a matter of having rules – no one reads lists of rules. How do we help people to implicitly know what sort of behavior is expected? Third, how do we react when someone knowingly or unknowingly violates those norms? And how do we do that *efficiently*? Give me enough money and I'll give you highly trained staff who will make sure everything is always perfect. On a realistic customer support budget, compromises are necessary.

Deciding what behavior is allowed and choosing tools and strategies to manage bad behavior are inseparable questions. The tools we have to regulate behavior shape what behavior is encouraged and discouraged. Social rules (written and unwritten) also shape behavior. The behavior that emerges then drives the development of both new tools for behavior management and new social norms and written rules for what behavior is acceptable. It's a complex socio-technical system (a combination of people, technologies, and social practices) that is continually evolving.

This chapter focuses primarily on bad behavior like harassment, hate speech, and content that people may find offensive. Deliberately posting something false – *disinformation* – is a form of bad behavior. Posting something that is false without realizing it is *misinformation*. For more on misinformation and what it means for something to be "false," see Chapter 3.

## What Regulates Behavior?

According to law professor Larry Lessig, four things regulate behavior: laws, social norms, technology/architecture, and markets (Lessig 1999, 87). As usual, we can start by thinking about face-to-face behavior and then draw analogies to online behavior. Lessig uses smoking behavior as his example. Laws regulate where you are allowed to smoke, and social norms dictate that it is rude to smoke in someone else's car without asking first. The technology of smoking – the addictive nature of nicotine – shapes how much people smoke. Finally, the market also shapes smoking behavior. Every time governments raise taxes on a pack of cigarettes, smoking in that area declines. These same factors – laws, social norms, technology, and markets – also shape online behavior (Lessig 1999). None of these factors are straightforward and they all affect one another. I'll talk about the first three factors in this chapter; markets are the topic of Chapter 7.

## Laws

Laws controlling what one may say (online or in other media) are complicated. In some countries, blasphemy is against the law (York 2012). In a few, the punishment for blasphemy is death. In many, it is illegal to criticize the government either by law or in practice.[1] In a few countries, such as Thailand, the law of Lèse-Majesté makes it illegal to criticize the royal family.

Although Americans put a high value on free speech, a surprising amount of speech is illegal under US law. Danielle Citron writes:

> Not all speech enjoys constitutional protection. Certain categories of speech can be regulated because they bring about serious harms and make only the slightest contribution to public debate. True threats are not immunized from regulation even though they may be conveyed in words. Defamation can be regulated consistent with our commitment to free speech. Obscenity does not enjoy constitutional protection even though it involves images. (Citron 2014, 26–27)

Those are just a few examples. I teach about this in my class "Computing, Society, and Professionalism," and students are often surprised. They know that, for example, slander and libel are illegal, and so is false advertising – but they hadn't thought about those as restrictions on speech. Existing, generally accepted restrictions on speech may be taken for granted as normal. There are many existing restrictions on speech in the United States. Citron points out that online speech is just as important as face-to-face speech. She writes that "Because the internet serves as people's workspaces,

---

[1] https://en.wikipedia.org/wiki/Freedom_of_speech_by_country

professional networks, résumés, social clubs, and zones of public conversation, it deserves the same protection as offline speech" (Citron 2014, 26).

"Hate speech" is legal in the United States, but illegal in many other nations. What is "hate speech," exactly? The United Nations defines hate speech as "any kind of communication in speech, writing or behaviour, that attacks or uses pejorative or discriminatory language with reference to a person or a group on the basis of who they are, in other words, based on their religion, ethnicity, nationality, race, colour, descent, gender or other identity factor" (United Nations n.d.). However, the details of how this is phrased matter, and the legal definition varies from place to place.

Some laws regulating speech are national, and others vary at the local level. Not only is what you can legally say in the United States different from what you can say in Australia,[2] but inside Australia what you can say in New South Wales is different from what you can say in Queensland.[3] To complicate things further, online speech typically has an international reach. Companies situated in one country often are forced either to develop content-screening mechanisms to comply with rules in other countries, or block access to their site from those countries.

An American approach suggests that it is a slippery slope to censor speech. When you pass laws saying that some things can't be said, where do you draw the line? Americans worry that speech restrictions could be

---

[2] https://en.wikipedia.org/wiki/Hate_speech
[3] https://en.wikipedia.org/wiki/Hate_speech_laws_in_Australia

manipulated for political ends. As a result, hate speech is legal. People who disapprove of certain speech are encouraged to counter it with other speech.

My earliest exposure to the dilemma of hate speech was in 1977, when I was eleven years old. That year, the US Supreme Court ruled that a group of neo-Nazis could march through a neighborhood in Skokie, Illinois, that had many Jewish residents including Holocaust survivors (*National Socialist Party of America* v. *Village of Skokie* 1977[4]). The court decided that the Nazis may march if they wish, but others who disagreed may come to counter-protest. I remember discussing this extensively with my stepfather, Bernie Zucker (who is an attorney), at the time, and it took me a while to understand the reasoning. The dilemma is that if the government decides that Nazis may not march, what other groups may not march? Who decides what groups are allowed, and how can we be sure this won't be used to silence dissent? To be on the safe side, American law allows as much speech as possible. It's a quintessentially American idea to privilege free speech to this degree.

In many other nations, hate speech is illegal – such as in the countries of the European Union, Canada, and many more. The Wikipedia page on the hate speech laws of different nations makes for fascinating reading (https://en .wikipedia.org/wiki/Hate_speech). Social media platforms and internet service providers often dedicate significant resources to complying with local laws. Some nations,

---

[4] www.oyez.org/cases/1976/76-1786

including Germany, levy fines on platforms that fail to take down illegal content. Others, such as China, simply block sites that don't meet their standards. To answer the question "is this content legal?" you need to know where the sender and receiver of the content are located.

Understanding what content is legal is only a first step toward understanding what content is allowed. Laws protecting free speech control whether the government can block speech, but do not apply to private platforms. In the United States, the government can't stop you, for example, from insulting a politician, but Reddit or Twitter legally can. It's like the distinction between a public park and a private home. In a public park, anyone can be present. In my home, I can decide who to let in and who to exclude. Similarly, an online site can decide what speech to exclude. They can't systematically discriminate against individuals in certain protected categories; however, beyond that they don't have to justify their decisions. An online site is more like a private party than a public square.

## How Could Laws About Speech be Improved?

Many laws about free speech pre-date internet technologies. Existing laws do not always adapt well to fundamentally different situations created by new technologies. For example, when the telephone was invented, the law in the United States was confused about whether a phone conversation had an expectation of privacy. If phone communication is public, then law enforcement may listen. If it's not public, can law enforcement ever ask for permission to listen? How would they request permission, and what are the grounds for saying yes or no?

The first telephone was invented in 1849. Over 100 years later, law enforcement tried to prosecute Charles Katz for illegal gambling based on evidence obtained in wiretaps of his phone. The court ruled that Katz had a reasonable expectation that his phone call was private, even though there was no physical trespass used to obtain the recording (Lessig 1999, 117). A year later, the Omnibus Crime and Safe Streets Act of 1968 made it legal for law enforcement to listen in on phone conversations if they got a warrant demonstrating probable cause. This solved the dilemma of whether to allow wiretapping by creating checks and balances between branches of government. This is an elegant solution. However, it took nearly 120 years for the law to catch up with the technology.

It's not surprising, then, that laws have not yet fully adapted to internet technologies. The earliest internet began in the 1960s. If it takes 120 years for the law to adapt as it did for the telephone, that would mean we can expect the beginnings of legal clarity by the 2080s! A more effective regulatory framework would give clearer guidance on what is legal to post online, whose responsibility it is to remove bad content, and how to operate in an international environment with divergent standards.

The current complexity of internet regulation gives an advantage to big companies compared to small ones. Large internet companies can afford to hire legal teams to figure out how to adapt their site to laws in different countries, and extra software developers to implement necessary regionalizations. Small companies don't have those resources; however, they sometimes benefit from having a low profile. A small website in the United States is, for example, unlikely to attract the attention of German regulators for failing to block hate speech in Germany.

The regulatory framework for speech in the United States is in need of improvement. There are two core problems. First, companies are profiting from hate. Large technology companies in the United States are earning advertising dollars from sharing and promoting speech that would be classified as "hate speech" in many nations. Those profits incentivize companies to continue sharing this content. Second, those companies can silence speech at their own discretion, with no accountability or recourse.

The power of corporations to make unilateral decisions about speech extends not just to social media platforms, but also to infrastructure companies such as domain name service registrars and cloud hosting platforms that other platforms rely on. Regulation at the infrastructure level can be challenging to circumvent. For example, in January 2021, Apple and Google removed the controversial app Parler from their online stores, and Amazon Web Services (AWS) stopped hosting the Parler website. Conversation on Parler helped organize the attack on the US Capitol on January 6, 2021, and many people were happy to see it shut down. The site was able to come back online a month later, but the shutdown still raises questions. York et al. (2021) comment on the Electronic Frontier Foundation blog:

Regardless of whether we agree with an individual decision, these decisions overall have not and will not be made democratically and in line with the requirements of transparency and due process, and instead are made by a handful of individuals, in a handful of companies, most distanced and least visible to most Internet users.
Whether you agree with those decisions or not, you will not be a part of them, nor be privy to their considerations. And unless we dismantle the increasingly centralized chokepoints in our global digital infrastructure, we can anticipate an escalating political battle between political factions and nation states to seize control of their powers.

American free speech laws were written with the idea that censorship is a slippery slope. You should not censor speech you disagree with, but rather counter it with other speech. In practice this has devolved into "the government can't censor speech, but private companies may do so." *We are not preventing censorship – just delegating the power.* I wonder whether the United States should move to more European-style speech laws, where standards for what may be said are debated by democratically elected representatives. The trade-offs are complicated.

With any set of rules for what speech is allowed, there will always be borderline and unprecedented cases that are hard to interpret. In 2020, Facebook created an "Oversight Board" to decide difficult cases for the platform. They have worked to try to make the board independent from Facebook. This corporate example might serve as a model for a comparable public board. We need democratic and transparent mechanisms both to establish policy for what content is allowed, and to manage edge cases where the established policies don't give clear guidance.

## Rules and Social Norms

Not all content that is legal is allowed. Platforms have written rules for what content is permitted that are typically much more restrictive than what is legal. Furthermore, people respond to social cues about what content is welcome for a particular venue.

Most sites have written rules for what sort of content is allowed. For commercial sites, some of the rules are defined in the site's terms of service (TOS), and those terms are a legally binding document. People don't typically read TOS – it would take too long for any person to read the TOS for all the sites they use, and the reading level is well above average (Fiesler et al. 2016; Jensen and Potts 2004). Terms of service are often referred to when a problem occurs, but rarely help new users understand norms because no one reads them.

You might assume that TOS are quite similar across sites, but they actually vary widely. In a study of the intellectual property part of terms of service on thirty sites where people share content they have created, Casey Fiesler, Cliff Lampe, and I found a surprising degree of variation. We found one site whose TOS grants the site an irrevocable, worldwide license to do whatever they want with all content uploaded without credit to the creator. Other sites were more reasonable. The legal terms are often quite different from what users expect and what they think is fair (Fiesler et al. 2016).

A site like Reddit has site-wide rules defined in the TOS and other posted policies, but also lets local groups (subreddits) add their own rules. Each subreddit has its own rules defined by its moderators. Even among groups on the same general topic, what you can say varies. For example, content allowed on r/science is quite different from what is allowed on r/askscience or r/sciences. The group r/science requires that all posts be peer-reviewed articles published in the last six months; the others are open to a wider variety of content as long as it's about scientific topics.

Nathan Matias found that if subreddits post their rules on their front page, people's compliance with those rules improves (Matias and Mou 2018). One of the nice things about Reddit is that if you don't like how a particular group is run, you can start your own – and then you're in charge of defining the rules. This fact is ethically critical. If there were only one place in the world to discuss an issue, then it would be problematic to say only certain things can be said there. On the other hand, if there are many competing forums, then it's easier to justify each one having its own local rules and excluding certain kinds of speech.

While lists of rules certainly play a significant role in regulating online behavior, much of how people learn how to behave in a given space is communicated in more subtle ways. In the face-to-face world, we learn that at an opera you are expected to sit quietly in your seat and applaud only at the end of the performance. On the other hand, at a sporting event, cheering and clapping can happen at any moment, and leaping out of your seat is appropriate. How do people learn to sit quietly at an opera and cheer loudly at a basketball game? As we saw in our discussion of Erving Goffman's work on presentation of self in Chapter 5, cues for how to behave are communicated by every detail of the setting – what the space looks like, who else is there, how people dress, and how those others are behaving. A venue may subtly or directly encourage a certain kind of behavior (such as an announcement on the jumbotron at a sporting event "Let's make some noise!"). People consciously and unconsciously read a host of cues, some prominent and some subtle.

Just as you learn how to behave at the opera by observing environmental cues, you also learn how to behave on Facebook by observing those cues. You see what kinds of things friends post on their newsfeeds or group members post in Facebook groups, and without consciously thinking about it you tend to post things that fit in. People learn what kind of content is allowed and what is appreciated through observation. Social norms emerge from behavior of the group.

## Online Groups, Civility, and Radicalization

Because social norms emerge from the behavior of online groups, those groups can foster civility or incivility. Two teams of students in my "Design of Online Communities" class have studied the YouTube channel of Shirley Curry, a grandmother who posts videos of herself playing the game *Skyrim*. In the comments on Curry's YouTube channel, everyone is incredibly polite. If a newcomer is rude, they are quickly corrected by the channel regulars – that's not how we behave here! Curry insists that even correcting someone who is being rude must be done in a polite fashion. The group has evolved social norms of politeness that are reinforced by both the group's leader and other members.

Just as good behavior among members of a group can be mutually reinforcing, the same is true of bad behavior. In our face-to-face lives, people may experience individual acts of hate speech. Groups engaging in hate speech together are thankfully less common. Online, however, the situation is different. An example is hate speech against fat[5] people. It happens all too often that someone makes a disparaging remark to a person who is fat. Such incidents primarily involve two people: a perpetrator and a victim. Now imagine a situation where a group of people all collectively start calling someone who is fat unkind names, and a bystander walking by listens for a moment and then joins in. This is a rare occurrence in the physical world, but a common one online – it's exactly what happened on the subreddit r/fatpeoplehate. People observing the online group quickly learned that insulting fat people is not only allowed in the group, but is rewarded. After an individual has observed such a group for a while, they may internalize those attitudes. Someone who hadn't really thought about the issue before may develop hateful views, and may express those views in other contexts both online and off. Group behavior can literally change people's beliefs – even their core beliefs on important issues.

---

[5] The fat acceptance movement recommends use of the word "fat" rather than medicalized terms like "obese" or "overweight."

What happens if we close those groups down? Reddit banned r/fatpeoplehate in 2015, and Eshwar Chandrasekharan, Eric Gilbert, and collaborators found that as a result there was less hate speech on all of Reddit. Former members of the hate subs r/fatpeoplehate and r/coontown (a racist group) did not continue the same sort of conversations elsewhere on Reddit – there was less hate speech in total (Chandrasekharan et al. 2017).

In a 1996 paper called "Finding One's Own Space in Cyberspace," I wrote that if you find yourself in a group that is not to your liking, you should simply find another group – or maybe start your own (Bruckman 1996). There's still an element of truth in that – not every group needs to be to your liking. But more than twenty-five years later, the issue looks more complicated to me. Foul online groups are contributing to people holding hateful views, and to the normalization of those views. Shutting down r/fatpeoplehate and r/coontown was the right thing for Reddit and for the world. The former members of those groups may have moved to other sites like Voat (which operated from 2014 to 2020), Parler, or Gab, where hate speech is expected and accepted. Actually tracing cross-platform movement is a challenging, unsolved research problem. Even if people did move to Gab and similar sites, those platforms are orders of magnitude smaller than Reddit, and much less likely to draw in new people who don't already share those hateful views.

This leads to a fundamental tension about freedom of speech: Who decides what is "foul"? It's tempting to adopt a perspective of cultural relativism – each group must decide what's acceptable for them. However, there are limits to cultural relativism. While it's better to err on the side of tolerance when you can, I'm willing to go out on a limb and say the views expressed on r/fatpeoplehate and r/coontown are *wrong*. American free speech laws mean that a platform is not required to restrict the expression of these views and if it chooses to accept them, this must be tolerated. In sum, this means that *platforms have an obligation to articulate their values*, and use those values to guide their design decisions on a daily basis. Rules and social norms on online platforms could be improved if platforms better articulate their values. Further, there is evidence that their decisions matter not just for them, but for the broader society. We are more hateful as a society because some online groups are encouraging hateful ideas.

## Technology

The next of Lessig's four modes of regulation is technology (Lessig 1999). Content moderation is typically accomplished by either software, humans, or "mixed-initiative" human–machine collaborations.

Lessig's core point is that code (software) embodies values. While we regulate things in person through laws, online it is often code that does the real regulation (Grimmelmann 2006; Lessig 1999). He contrasts the early campus networks at Harvard and University of Chicago. Harvard's network design from the start prioritized security and was strictly locked down – you needed to register your computer to connect. Chicago's campus network was more flexible and prioritized free speech – anyone could have access. Specific choices about how to implement each network embodied priorities and values. Those different goals led to quite different experiences for users of those networks. Similarly, as we make choices about how to moderate online content, all our choices are heavily value laden. Those choices are often not just expressed in code, but *created by* the code. The affordances of software – what is easy to do and what is hard – are inextricable from decisions by platform owners about what sorts of speech to permit.

Some automated systems for content regulation are simple. Shagun Jhaver, Eric Gilbert, and I studied Reddit's "Automod" tool, and found a number of strengths and weaknesses (Jhaver et al. 2019). Automod uses simple regular expression matching to decide what posts to remove. Sets of rules are curated by human moderators. If you give it a list of swear words, it can remove posts containing those words. These rules are dumb – they are just hard-coded patterns. For example, in moderating comments on r/coronavirus, I recently had to re-approve a comment that said "Alexandria Ocasio-Cortez graduated cum laude from Boston University." Automod had deleted it because "cum" is on the list of obscene words.

The specific implementation of those rules is often not revealed to users, because transparency enables gaming the system. If I ban a swear word, a user simply needs to misspell it to get it past the filter. Then I ban the misspelling, and then the user simply misspells it differently. Stevie Chancellor documented the lexical evolution that occurred when Instagram started trying to ban words related to pro-anorexic posts (Chancellor et al. 2016). Since keyword blocking starts an arms race of lexical variation and blocking, many sites choose not to tell users what words are blocked. A user is simply told their post was removed because it was inappropriate, and not that it was removed because it matched a forbidden string of characters. As a result, transparency is a paradox. Users want transparency – before I invest time in creating content, I want to know if it's allowed. Likewise, site managers want to clearly communicate what is allowed to users, to lessen the amount of content they need to remove. However, managers can't communicate the rules too clearly or it enables gaming the system.

Computers are currently not very good at nuanced judgment, although they are very good at pattern matching. Current advances in computer vision rely on matching an image to large databases of images. If the computer has a million pictures of dogs, it can evaluate a picture and see if it is a dog – does it look like those million dog pictures? This approach is called "machine learning" (ML), and a particularly powerful variant is "deep learning."

Computer vision is particularly good at removing bad images from online sites. It's possible now, for example, to create a reliable nudity detector, and remove nude images automatically if desired. This is an impressive feat – particularly if you consider the subtle differences between photos of people in scanty swimwear and photos that are defined as nudity.

The same techniques used for images can also be used on text. To detect hate speech, I can compare it to hate speech I've collected and see if they match. However, the problem is fundamentally harder. Asking "is this offensive?"

is subtler than asking "is this a dog?" In fact, given a particular utterance, two humans may have trouble coming to agreement on whether it is hate speech or content that is appropriate for a given online venue.

One challenge for ML approaches is the quality of input data. My colleague Judy Hoffman notes that you can't really make a dog detector by simply gathering lots of pictures of dogs that people share online. That makes a very good front-facing dog detector. People generally don't post pictures of their dogs from behind (or other angles), so recognition software built from owners' photos fails miserably unless the dog is facing you. Machine learning doesn't generalize well to unseen examples. Datasets for matching may be too small, or systematically biased (Hoffman et al 2017; Saenko et al. 2010).

The same is true for datasets for identifying hate speech. You need a lot of bad speech to start matching well, and what is "bad" can also be contextual in complicated ways. Eshwar Chandrasekharan and colleagues found that there are social norms on Reddit that apply to the whole site (macro), to significant parts of the site (meso), and other norms that are more purely local (micro) (Chandrasekharan et al. 2018). These three levels likely exist on most sites, and we haven't yet developed effective tools to automatically detect content violations at the macro, meso, or micro levels.

A critical challenge for ML technology is explainability. Most ML approaches can broadly say "this looks like the bad content you gave me," but can't yet give a human-understandable explanation for *why* a specific piece of content is not acceptable. This creates problems for people who need to decide when to trust ML systems, and is a barrier to designing effective mixed-initiative human–machine decision systems.

## Enacting Moderation: Software, Volunteers, and Staff

In most content moderation systems, software does a first-pass review of online content, makes decisions on easy cases, and passes harder decisions to humans to review. It is a human–machine partnership. Each stage of this process has room for improvement. To begin, platforms could do a better job of articulating policies, and setting up both software and human systems charged with enacting them. Machines could make better decisions about content and make better choices about what to send for human review. Humans charged with enacting policy could do a better job of doing so consistently and fairly.

For the human role, sites use different mixes of volunteer and paid labor. It's a fascinating question why volunteers choose to do so much unpaid work in the service of corporations. In Chapter 2 I explored the motivations that encourage people to contribute to collaborative online content creation in citizen science and open-source software. Volunteers enjoy the feeling that they are contributing to something meaningful, and also appreciate the sense of community in the group. Similarly, volunteer moderators typically care about the groups they are shepherding, and enjoy the elevated status their role gives them. In some cases, there is a strong sense of comradery among volunteers, and they volunteer time in a spirit of supporting the group. As we saw in Chapter 2, people often invest time in online groups because they reap social and psychological rewards.

In the 1990s, early volunteer moderators on America Online received free accounts. America Online was one of the first online services to achieve mass adoption. Its early service was dial-up – connecting required a modem and a phone line – and users were charged by the hour. It was possible at that time to run up an expensive bill if you were connected too many hours. Consequently, a totally free, unlimited account was a significant perk for volunteer mods. In 1995, AOL moved to a flat monthly fee of $15.95 for unlimited connection time for everyone. However, they still expected volunteer moderators to work a specified number of hours to maintain their free accounts (Postigo 2003). A perk that previously might have been worth hundreds of dollars or more per month was suddenly worth $15.95. In 1999, a group of moderators sued AOL, stating that they were being treated as employees and paid lower than minimum wage. The case was settled a decade later for $15 million (Kirchner 2011). It's an interesting historical moment because it shows early tensions about who volunteer moderators are, what their relationship to the corporation is, and why they volunteer their time.

Paid workers in the space of content moderation fall into two primary groups: high-paid workers who help set policy and make key difficult decisions, and low-paid workers who look at offensive content in volume and make quick decisions. The low-paid workers are often located in the Global South, where wages are extremely low. Sara

T. Roberts studies the working conditions for these workers, and finds many work for long hours looking at disturbing content, and may suffer serious psychological harm (Roberts 2017). These commercial content moderation workers receive varied levels of training, and guidelines with varied clarity. Further, their work is often not audited for compliance with guidelines, and some workers may impose their own values rather than following the guidelines they've been given (Radiolab 2018).

Taken together, content moderation requires a complex combination of people, policies, social practices, and tools. These components are interdependent in every possible way. For example, the nature of the tools shapes the basic policies that are established – you do what it is easy or possible to do. The nature of the tools also shapes the actions people take. Important decisions emerge from this web of interdependencies in complex and sometimes unpredictable ways.

## An Ounce of Prevention

While we can remove inappropriate content once it has been posted, an even better approach is to discourage people from posting bad content in the first place. People who violate social norms sometimes do so on purpose, often for their amusement. Whitney Phillips documents the psychology of "trolls" who deliberately provoke others "for the lulz" (Phillips 2015). We saw in Chapter 2 that collaborative work online becomes much more difficult if some participants are trying to deliberately disrupt it. In contrast, a significant amount of content that breaches social norms is shared simply because the posters didn't understand expectations. Designers can work to establish shared expectations among users, and this can significantly reduce the amount of bad behavior and bad content. Dealing with bad content that is created intentionally and unintentionally are quite different challenges.

Different kinds of groups have different degrees of content and behavior problems. First, keeping a group small and low-profile can reduce attention from people who don't buy into the goals of the group. If you are the largest or the most important place to discuss a particular topic, lots of people will be attracted to the forum. A smaller group is less likely to attract disruptive individuals. A more humbly packaged group is less likely to attract disruptive people than one that declares its own importance. As we discussed in Chapter 1, this is analogous to Ray Oldenburg's observation that some third places use plainness as a "protective coloration" (Oldenburg 1989).

Second, for discussion forums, the sensitivity of the topic changes how much controversial behavior is likely to emerge. A space devoted to controversial topics like politics or abortion is more likely to become heated than, for example, one devoted to a hobby like knitting or hiking.

Over time, some spaces tend to be friendly (like Shirley Curry's YouTube channel) and others (like the online games *Overwatch* and *League of Legends*) tend to have toxic atmospheres. The fascinating question for designers is: What factors lead to a more or less toxic culture emerging?

## Online Public Shaming

Bad behavior is not just an individual act – it emerges from groups. I've talked about how members of a group can encourage one another to engage in bad behavior. Groups can also facilitate bad outcomes in another way: the sheer volume of behavior can be problematic. Something can be appropriate if one person says it, or even if ten people say it – but problematic if a hundred or a thousand people say it. Even if each of those people's statements, taken alone, is unproblematic, the total volume of communication can become harassment.

Consider the case of online public shaming. Sometimes it's appropriate to give people critical feedback. The internet excels at helping individuals to speak out against abusive policies of corporations, or bad behavior by individuals. However, this process can go too far. Sometimes one person's behavior provokes a viral response that goes well beyond what is warranted in the situation. For example, in June 2005 a young woman's dog defecated on a subway in South Korea. She refused to clean up her dog's mess, and a witness took her picture and posted it online. Her identity was uncovered by people on the internet after her photo was widely shared.[6]

What punishment did this woman deserve? You might think she should pay a fine. A stronger consequence would require her to do hours of public service cleaning the subway. What actually happened is that she was so

---

[6] https://en.wikipedia.org/wiki/Dog_poop_girl

bombarded with online attacks that she dropped out of her university. That is excessive. Someone telling the dog owner that her behavior was rude was appropriate. The problem comes when *everyone* tells her. And when the long-term consequences spiral out of control.

The activity that began this incident (the woman failing to clean up after her dog) had nothing to do with the internet, but what followed next could not have happened without computer-mediated communications. In other situations, the precipitating event happens online. For a detailed account of one example, journalist Jon Ronson's article "How One Stupid Tweet Blew Up Justine Sacco's Life" is a compelling read (Ronson 2015). There are a growing number of examples of internet public shaming that have had out-of proportion consequences.

## Computer-Generated Content

The final assignment for my "Design of Online Communities" class is a two-page reflection on "how you think online communities, social media, and the internet, will be different ten years from now." In spring 2020, PhD student Daniel Nkemelu submitted this (reproduced with permission):

> *Ten years from now, social media will* remain the primary
> means by which we discover, create and share
> information. Indeed, it will be necessary to have more
> than a highly specialized technical skill set to be an
> effective journalist, which means the work of this century
> will demand a distinctly different approach to the craft of
> journalism. With this in mind, and the recent

developments of the Internet, the Boston Globe's Jim Yardley issued a terse "call to arms" in The Boston Globe on December 20, 2008 (courtesy of Techdirt): We'll soon be turning into a world of social media – where the most important player in the communication revolution will be one which is already a billion dollar industry: Facebook. *Also, the internet will provide interesting challenges and opportunities.* First, the search for intellectual ideas is the major philosophical enterprise of our day, and it has to take place online, since so few people have the ability to visit a library, get hold of an encyclopedia or participate in a scholarly conversation. Yet new resources, like Wikipedia, allow everyone to participate in these discussions, contributing their thoughts and to come up with new content. Finally, the links between different networks on the web will also help to disseminate knowledge. Here, we see the general principle that the outside world will become our channels of communication and, if we can be really successful, serve as the nodes for more significant social communication.

If it is not obvious already, everything posted up to this point has been spewed by Open AI's GPT-2 Transformer-based model which generates synthetic text samples in response to the model being seeded with some leading statements. Only the sentences in italics were written by me. In fact, with a little more effort from me, these synthetic sentences would become harder to detect. As I reflected on how social media and the internet will change in a decade, I am reminded of how unprepared today's platforms are for the influx of new automated actors running engines powered by models like GPT-2.

Nkemelu is right: We are woefully under-prepared for the coming influx of automatically generated content. That content can be in any media. Much recent research has focused on detecting fake videos or "deep fakes." Videos started circulating on the internet in 2018 showing public figures saying things they never said (Schwartz 2018). This will be used to manipulate the public in scary ways. Chesney and Citron write:

> The marketplace of ideas already suffers from truth decay as our networked information environment interacts in toxic ways with our cognitive biases. Deep fakes will exacerbate this problem significantly. Individuals and businesses will face novel forms of exploitation, intimidation, and personal sabotage. The risks to our democracy and national security are profound as well. (Chesney and Citron 2018, 1754)

Modifying video will leave evidence of manipulation that can be detected in the data, so programs will often be able to identify videos as inauthentic. There will likely be an "arms race" between generation programs and detection programs, each becoming more sophisticated over time. However, even if detection of fake video works perfectly, we still face the issue of whether people will pay attention to annotations and whether they will believe the video is real or fake. Automatically generated text, such as in Daniel's assignment, may be even harder to detect, though possibly less problematic in its impact than video.

There are many positive uses of synthetic media. For example, we can generate realistic dialog for truly interactive training simulations and narrative games. There have been intriguing applications of synthetic video to complete movies when an actor has died in the middle of filming. (Though this does raise thorny legal issues about the possible future use and misuse of people's likenesses.) Synthetic dialog is of course needed for anthropomorphic digital assistants and robots. While these applications have great potential, a big impact of synthetic media going forward is going to be a need to invest tremendous amounts of research time (and money) in ever-more-sophisticated ways to detect it. As Daniel Nkemelu notes, we are not ready.

## Exit, Voice, and Loyalty

The presence of harassment and inappropriate content online reflect a decline in the quality of a platform. In his classic book *Exit, Voice, and Loyalty*, Albert Hirschman argues that customers who are displeased with a product or service have two potential responses (Hirschman 1970). First, they can leave. This is "exit," and is an economic strategy. As customers leave, they put pressure on the organization to improve their quality.

An alternative to leaving is to express their dissatisfaction to the management. This is "voice," a political strategy. Voice requires more effort than exit (in most situations), and is more uncertain. You can invest effort in speaking up but see no benefit. Writing in 1970 (when the internet was still just a small research network at a few universities), Hirschman comments that "the creation of effective new channels through which consumers can communicate their dissatisfaction" (Hirschman 1970, 78) will raise the value of voice as a response. The internet provides new channels beyond what Hirschman could have imagined. Social networks like Twitter have given the public remarkable new ways to exercise their voice.

Exit and voice shape each other. Hirschman points out that it is often the most quality-conscious consumers who exit, which undermines voice. For example, if everyone who cares about education moves their children to private schools, then the public schools have lost their most vocal advocates for quality. Similarly, if everyone who cares about their privacy left Facebook after various privacy scandals, then Facebook would lose its most vocal advocates of quality.

Hirschman's third concept is loyalty. Loyalty "holds exit at bay and activates voice" (Hirschman 1970, 78). The three concepts – exit, voice, and loyalty – all affect one another in a kind of ecology.

The model is made more complicated by the fact that people disagree on the nature of "quality." Suppose two groups have competing visions for a product. The company might choose to compromise between those visions. However, if one group is more likely to exit, then the response may favor their preference. The dynamics are interesting. Apply this model, for example, to an online platform that has a group that prefers a stricter version of free speech versus a group that prefers greater protection from harassment and misinformation. To balance their interests, the platform might ask, how numerous is each subgroup? Who is more likely to leave in frustration? How vocal is each subgroup? Are the vocal members an accurate reflection of the views of silent members or are the members making demands really outliers? Hirschman's model gives us some tools to think through this dilemma. If the platform is driven simply by the goal of maximizing site participation and profits, then they have complicated calculations about how far to go to please each side. On the other hand, if they are driven by values about what sort of discourse they aim to support, then the calculation is simpler.

Reddit provides an example of exit and voice functioning well together. Reddit is organized into millions of subreddits, and anyone can start a new one. When user u/sirt6 was frustrated with strict policies on r/science, he founded a new subreddit called r/sciences, which quickly grew to have over 100,000 subscribers. It's easy to exit a subgroup of Reddit without exiting the platform as a whole, which is to the strategic advantage of the management. Voice operates well on Reddit when the volunteer moderators on subreddits are responsive to users. A complaint is likely to get a human response and maybe even discussion (depending on how big the subreddit is and how well managed). Contrast this to the feeling you get when you send a complaint to central management of Twitter or Facebook. In those cases, after a long delay you typically get what feels like a form letter response. When voice feels pointless, users are more likely to resort to exit. Hirschman's book in many ways feels like it was written to help us understand the internet.

## Value Judgments

Ultimately everything about online content management is about values. What kind of site do I want to create, and what kind of world am I helping create through it? One of those values is free speech. However, that is balanced against other values – like the right to be free from harassment. Balancing these demands is challenging. It's fortunate that there is not just one online space – we can create different spaces that deal with these trade-offs in different ways.

## Theoretical Summary

Policies for what kind of content is allowed and social and technical mechanisms for enforcing those policies are inextricably intertwined. Things that regulate behavior include laws, social norms, and technology (Lessig 1999). Each of these factors is complicated to understand, and the ways we use each has significant room for improvement.

Governments are often slow to adapt laws to suit new technologies like the internet. Laws about what content is allowed differ not only at the national, but even at the local level. One of the most hotly contested questions is the formal definition of "hate speech" and whether hate speech is allowed. In most countries, hate speech is illegal. In the United States, because we fear censorship, hate speech is allowed. While the First Amendment to the US Constitution says the government can't restrict your right to free speech, private platforms are not bound by this and may impose any restrictions they choose.

Rules for behavior are sometimes defined by explicit lists of rules (like TOS). More often, however, social norms emerge from the behavior of the group. People learn by observing others' behavior. Designers of online sites create conditions that subtly shape user behavior, hoping certain kinds of behavior will emerge.

Inappropriate content can be viewed as a decline in quality of the online service. Consumers displeased with such content have two key strategies to respond: exit (leaving the platform, an economic strategy) and voice (expressing their displeasure, a political strategy). If people are loyal to a platform, they are more likely to use voice and less likely to use exit. The dynamic relationship between exit, voice, and loyalty can help us understand online platforms and their struggle to manage content.

## Practical Implications

Laws, social norms, and technology work together to regulate online behavior. One more factor – markets – is the topic of Chapter 7. Regulating online behavior, at the time I am writing, seems like an impossibly hard challenge – something that is broken about the internet. The way to improve the situation is to focus on each of the four factors, and their inter-relations.

Platforms can carefully balance the desires of different subgroups with regard to issues like free speech and protection from harassment and misinformation. However, trying to please both sides can create situations where no one is happy. An alternative approach is for platforms to articulate guiding values. In other words, one site might say, "you may say anything here," and another may say, "you must be civil here, according to our definition of civility." However, this is only equitable if viable alternate platforms exist for those with competing values.

We can "let a thousand flowers bloom" – that is, have sites with all different sorts of standards, and let each person find the one best suited to them. It remains a hard question whether there is some speech that is so extreme that it should not be tolerated anywhere. The challenge is who gets to decide what counts as too extreme. For example, there are places in the world today where espousing atheist views is still a serious crime. For that reason, I believe that all speech, no matter how extreme, should be tolerated somewhere. However, segregating that speech to its own zones can lessen its negative impact and help reduce its "contagious" nature.

# 7   How Do Business Models Shape Online Communities?

You can't understand technology in isolation – it is inseparable from the social systems that create it, and in which it is used. Researchers in human–computer interaction (HCI) study technology embedded in the world, thinking about "socio-technical systems." Dix et al. write that "Socio-technical models are concerned with technical, social, organizational, and human aspects of design. They recognize the fact that technology is not developed in isolation but part of a wider organizational environment. It is therefore important to consider social and technical issues side by side" (Dix et al. 1998, 224). Financial factors often don't receive enough attention as a component of the socio-technical system. In this chapter, I will argue that markets are a critical component of that broader social environment. *How things are financed changes what they become.*

The original computer network that later became the internet, the ARPANET, was created as a research project funded by the US Department of Defense (Clark 2018). Today, the internet (from the physical layer up to the application layer) is partly funded by governments and partly by companies. A number of smaller online platforms (like Mattermost and Mastodon) are non-profit, but most are run by corporations and supported either by advertising or subscription fees. How online sites are funded profoundly shapes them.

In this chapter, I will focus on three fundamental ways in which financial factors shape content moderation and online interaction. First, if there is a cost for joining a site or participating in a site, this shapes who can afford it, and who chooses to afford it. Second, customer service is expensive. How we manage bad behavior is fundamentally shaped by how much it costs. Third, how sites make money shape their priorities, design decisions, and policies.

## Markets as a Regulator

As we saw in the last chapter, Larry Lessig describes four things that regulate behavior: laws, social norms, technology, and markets. To explain the impact of markets on behavior, Lessig uses the example of smoking. Raising cigarette taxes lowers the number of people who smoke. Markets are a classic way to regulate behavior, and it works for online behavior just like face-to-face behaviors.

Today, people are accustomed to most online sites being free. On supposedly "free" sites, users are often paying by allowing their personal information to be mined, and by accepting targeted advertising. When there is a fee to participate, even a token fee can dramatically reshape user behavior. One of the first community networks, Berkeley Community Memory, leveraged this technique with great success. Faced with a deluge of low-quality posts, they began charging a small fee – just 25 cents – for each post. As a result, the quality of content on the site improved (Shuler 1994). In earlier chapters we discussed peer review as a powerful force for ensuring quality of content. This small fee encouraged self-review, which is also powerful.

Small fees can have big impacts. The irreverent online discussion site the Something Awful Forums (SAF, www.somethingawful.com) prides itself on its high-quality discussion. New users are represented by an icon that says "stupid newbie" unless they pay a small one-time fee (formerly $5, now $9.95) for a paid account. This simple filter helps raise the level of conversation (Pater et al. 2014).

One nice side-effect of the small fee to join SAF is that it makes people think twice about bad behavior. On most online sites, if your account is banned you can just create a new one. Some subreddits try to counter that by blocking submissions from accounts that were created too recently, or have low karma (points you get for upvotes on your posts and comments). On SAF, the fee to join is an elegant deterrent. If you get yourself banned, it's going to cost you $9.95 to come back!

A larger fee, of course, has a bigger impact. In the face-to-face world, many social clubs use high or extremely high fees to filter potential members. Clubs with high fees become places for elites to socialize. Such clubs play a role in reproducing inequality – when members of elites network, they inevitably help one another, which reinforces privilege. Not surprisingly, such elite clubs are being created online. For example, the site Rich Kids (https://richkids.life) charges €1,000 per month for membership, and promises that tabloids will see your photos. The site Whispers is only for owners of new Rolls Royce cars (Mihalascu 2020). I'm sure there are many sites with expensive barriers to entry that are not visible to the public. An elite country club has a physical footprint that passers-by can see, but digital ones can be invisible to outsiders.

Market forces like subscription fees may be key to managing bad content on the internet in the future. Over the last few years, there has been a growing recognition that much content on the internet is problematic. In his science fiction book *Fall; or, Dodge in Hell* (Stephenson 2019), author Neal Stephenson imagines a world in which individuals hire editors to manage content they see. Poor people use automated programs to filter their content, and thousands of people may use the same filter. Rich people, on the other hand, hire human editors who know their likes and interests and tailor an information feed for them personally. The result is that people who are economically advantaged get access to better information. In Stephenson's dystopian vision, reliable information is a privilege of the rich, and the less advantaged often sink into bizarre conspiracy and cult beliefs encouraged by a steady flow of unreliable information. With the current rise in belief in false conspiracies like QAnon, chemtrails, and a flat earth, Stephenson's prediction is increasingly plausible.

During the Middle Ages through much of the Renaissance, information was indeed the privilege of the rich. Wealthy merchants hired staff at great expense to go to court and report back on what was taking place. The advent of the first newspapers in the seventeenth century began a gradual process of making news available to a broader segment of society (Pettegree 2014). Wikipedia is the high point of this trend, making the world's knowledge more accessible than ever before.

Some of the first newspapers were sensationalist tabloids, created with the primary goal of making money and only a secondary goal of informing or enlightening. Information that is commercially available has long been of mixed quality (Pettegree 2014). The problem of how to encourage the spread of good content and discourage the spread of bad is longstanding. At the time I am writing this, it feels like the problem is becoming more acute.

Market-based regulation mechanisms are likely to play a significant role in holding back the tide of bad content. How to achieve this without making better-quality information the privilege of the economically more advantaged is difficult and important.

## The Cost of Customer Service

A second way that financial factors regulate online behavior is the cost of customer service. For many sites, customer service is their second-largest non-fixed cost (after paying for bandwidth). How much content regulation is affordable fundamentally shapes what kinds of sites are possible.

This was particularly evident in the United States after the passage of the Children's Online Privacy Protection Act (COPPA) in 1998 (FTC 2020). Before this legislation, companies were requiring children to give away personal information as a precondition of playing online games. COPPA ruled that you could only ask kids for personal information with parental consent. Getting parental consent costs money – employees need to be hired to provide customer support for the process. After the law took effect, many sites for kids closed because their business models were no longer viable. New sites slowly opened over the next several years. In the end, sites for kids evolved into two groups: simple sites supported by advertising dollars that collect no personal information from kids, and more complex sites supported by subscription fees. The subscription fees help defray the cost of verifying parental consent. Changes in required customer support and level of content regulation reshaped the landscape of what sites for kids exist in a fundamental way. All of this is also true in sites for adults.

Data on how much companies spend on customer service is typically proprietary, but the story of Yahoo Answers gives some insight. In the late 2000s, developers at the question-and-answer site Yahoo Answers had a problem with growing amounts of offensive content. Hiring customer service representatives to manage content was costing a million dollars a year, and it was taking on average eighteen hours to respond to complaints.

Randy Farmer and colleagues came up with a clever solution: They built a reputation system for site members who report bad content. If a member has a history of correctly reporting bad content, then Yahoo Answers trusts that person and takes down content they report immediately. The person who posted the content can file an appeal to dispute the removal if they wish. Those appeals are handled by a customer service representative. If an appeal is successful, it lowers the reliable reporting reputation of the person who reported it. Yahoo can tell who to trust to make accurate reports.

When the system was launched, Yahoo found that few post removals were repealed – the people posting offensive content knew an appeal wouldn't be successful. As a result of this system, the average time it took to manage complaints went down from eighteen hours to *thirty seconds*, and the cost to Yahoo went from a million dollars a year to less than $10,000 a year, total. Farmer and Bryce Glass speculate that part of their jaw-dropping results was a sort of "broken window effect" – trolls quickly learned that Yahoo Answers was no longer a fun place to breach norms because the content would be removed so quickly (Farmer and Glass 2010). This solution leverages human intelligence rather than artificial intelligence. It simultaneously creates a new way to volunteer to help the site and empowers users. It's a clever way to reduce the cost of customer service.

In 1994, I organized a panel discussion at the ACM Computer–Human Interaction (CHI) conference on "Approaches to Managing Deviant Behavior in Virtual Communities." In the panel proposal, I very sincerely wrote that I advocated a psychological approach to managing bad behavior. An administrator having a serious heart-to-heart chat with someone who is annoying others could solve the problem in a deeper sense than just sanctioning them (Bruckman et al. 1994). In one sense, I wasn't wrong – that approach really can help solve underlying problems in a more lasting way. However, with the scale of today's internet, the suggestion is absurd. Volunteer moderators don't have time to devote minutes, much less hours, to each incident, and staff moderators cost money. Software programs are less expensive than human staff.

With unlimited funds, truly outstanding content moderation is possible. If I can hire enough paid staff and train them well, I can handle difficult content with speed and finesse. With a realistic budget, the situation is different. I organized another panel discussion at CHI on the same topic twelve years later in 2006 (and again in 2018). Reviewing what we knew in 2006 that we didn't know in 1994, a key observation was the fundamentally financial nature of the challenge (Bruckman et al. 2006).

What sort of behavior is allowed fundamentally shapes what a site becomes. Behavior management is shaped by the software systems and human workers (paid and volunteer) who manage it. Both software and human labor cost money. Even using volunteer labor, you need to invest money to pay administrators to respond to volunteer concerns, and build tools for volunteers to use. To understand the management of online behavior, you need to appreciate the connections between the social, technical, and financial aspects.

## The Evolution of Business Models
## for Online Communities

The third way that markets regulate online content is through the business models that support platforms. All the syllabi for my "Design of Online Communities" class are online, from 1998 to the present. I enjoy looking at past years and thinking about how my knowledge and the field's knowledge have evolved. One of the things that has changed the most over the years are the business models. The things I taught my class about topics like community and identity in 1998 still broadly hold true today. But I couldn't have told you much about future business models to support the internet. Those business models drive site design, so they're of central importance.

The evolution of the business model of Cartoon Network is a good example. Turner Broadcasting is near Georgia Tech, and Chris Waldron from Turner and Cartoon Network came to give guest lectures in my online communities class for many years. In the late 1990s when he first visited, online ads generated negligible revenue for Cartoon Network. Their revenue came from television ads and merchandising. Ads on the website were initially free if you purchased a television ad. The idea of targeted advertising wasn't yet generally understood. Today, online ads are a significant source of revenue for Cartoon Network and much of the technology sector of the economy.

A fundamental assumption behind our market-based economy is that consumers will make rational decisions in selecting products and services. Companies that provide quality products at a fair price will thrive, and others will fail. In this model, everyone simply needs to look out for themselves, and the magic power of the market will ensure that good things will happen. Except that our actual markets are fairly far from idealized markets, and things don't really turn out that way. The current state of the internet is an example.

## Business Models as Regulation

Commercial internet sites are driven primarily by the profit motive. Since the 1970s, it's been fashionable in financial circles to argue that publicly traded companies have an obligation to their stockholders to "maximize shareholder value" (Zuboff 2019). This is neoliberalism, "an ideology of unswerving loyalty to the logic of the market" (Field 2019, 5). Stock in those corporations is likely in your retirement fund, so the idea that they might try to thrive financially has merit. However, if that is their *only* guiding light, it leads to problems.

Underlying this ideology is the assumption that making financial gain the top priority is a kind of objective function that removes bias from the system. In other words, what makes the most money is the right choice for the economy and society. There is no evidence that this is true.

Consider the case of the YouTube recommendation algorithm. To make the most money, YouTube designed their algorithm to try to maximize each person's time on the site – so they would see the most advertisements. They discovered that leading people to more and more niche content and more controversial content keeps them on the site longer. This increases revenue from advertisements. That sounds like a reasonable design choice until you learn that much of that more-specific content advocates conspiracy theories and ideas not supported by mainstream science. Zeynep Tufecki notes that a simple search for mainstream political figures led her to conspiracy videos claiming that the attacks on the United States in September 2001 were perpetrated by the government. The algorithm quickly takes people to low-quality content, such as videos promoting false conspiracy theories and hate groups. You can maximize shareholder value better if you encourage people to watch extremist content – it can be quite engrossing. Tufekci concludes that "YouTube leads viewers down a rabbit hole of extremism, while Google racks up the ad sales" (Tufekci 2018). By maximizing profits, YouTube became an engine for convincing people of crazy nonsense.

The driving goal of YouTube and similar platforms is to show people more ads. The more you know about individuals, the more you can both keep them on your site and also better target ads to them. Shoshana Zuboff calls the business model of gathering trace data of people's online behavior for the purpose of targeted marketing "surveillance capitalism." In her book *The Age of Surveillance Capitalism*, she points out that many sites deliberately manipulate people to reveal more and more about themselves, for the purpose of marketing to them. As a result, she argues that companies like YouTube are treating people as means to an end – not as ends in themselves. This is *the definition of unethical* (the second formulation of the categorical imperative) as articulated by philosopher Immanuel Kant (Kant and Patton 1964). In the YouTube example, they are trying to maximize ad views without any thought to the impact of false content on individuals or society (Zuboff 2019).

In surveillance capitalism, companies gain more and more knowledge about individuals. Zuboff comments that "unequal knowledge about us produces unequal power over us, and so epistemic inequality widens to include the distance between what we can do and what can be done to us" (Zuboff 2020).

Some targeted advertising may be useful, but letting the desire to do better targeted advertising *drive the design of the entire system* is leading to bad outcomes for us as consumers and citizens. One possible solution to this dilemma is for companies to *better articulate and prioritize corporate values.* YouTube's mission statement says their goal is "to give everyone a voice and show them the world." It would be better if they aimed to show people the world *as it really is* – to spread knowledge. As we saw in Chapter 3, "knowledge" is justified, true belief. YouTube has begun to make constructive changes to the platform by no longer recommending content about conspiracies (Rosenblatt 2019) and banning misinformation related to public health (BBC 2020).

If platforms better articulate their values, then users can ideally choose among alternatives and select sites that appeal to them. If YouTube decides that they are going to prioritize "good" content, then they are in the uncomfortable position of having to decide what good content is. If there is only one platform, then it makes sense for it to allow all sorts of content. But you can imagine a world in which there is a marketplace of venues with different content policies, and then each person can choose a site that suits them. This already exists to some extent, but there aren't yet enough alternatives. When a few big sites dominate, there is no marketplace.

Another critical problem is that the values of existing platforms are often not clearly expressed to members. Some politically radical sites have been founded with clearly stated, explicit values. This has the benefit that users know what to expect. If you go on the alt-right site Gab and post in favor of liberal ideas (like advocating free college tuition or government-funded health insurance), you would expect to be downvoted or maybe even banned. Some of my students have tried it, and that's what happened! Where things get fraught is when users don't have clear expectations for what is allowed on a site, and then are surprised by a content removal. ("What do you mean I can't say that here?!")

Even if a platform tries not to have specific values, they end up being forced to make hard decisions. For example, in 2016 Facebook removed a photo of a naked nine-year-old girl and banned the person who posted it. Without more detail, that seems not only reasonable but mandatory. However, the specific photo was the 1972 Pulitzer-Prize-winning photo of a girl in Vietnam burned by napalm. The photo is historically significant and catalyzed a shift in American opinion about the war. Protests arose in response to the removal and the photo was restored (Shahani 2016). If it's hard to decide whether to allow a photo that is already widely recognized as historically important, imagine how hard the decision will be when the next shocking but important photo emerges. As Tarleton Gillespie eloquently documents in his book *Custodians of the Internet*, there is no way today for platforms to avoid hard decisions (Gillespie 2018). These decisions might be easier if corporations articulated a vision for their impact on the world more nuanced than maximizing shareholder value.

In 2020, Facebook launched an "Oversight Board" to help it make such hard decisions in the future, and is aiming for that board to function independently (FTC 2020).

This approach is promising and it will be interesting to see if it functions as hoped, and if other companies follow suit.

An advertising business model pressures platforms to maximize time on the platform and hence ad views. On the other hand, a flat fee, subscription-based business model means it benefits the platform financially if people participate just enough to love it and feel they get value, but no more (since usage incurs bandwidth and support costs). It's intriguing to consider what other business models are viable, and how those would shape incentives for platforms and users.

As we have seen, the business model of a site shapes its content policies. It also shapes where the site invests its precious, scarce development time for software engineers. What a site becomes depends on what its leaders value, and the bottom line can dominate executives' thinking. A bit more attention to what kind of world a site is creating would help. My optimistic hope is that sites that pay more attention to values will actually make more money in the long run. People switch to the email provider ProtonMail because it preserves privacy and security. We need lots more ProtonMails – alternative sites guided by values.

## What New Business Models Are Possible?

We have not yet invented all the forms of online community. Some of them we may stumble into. In fact, the collaboration platform Slack began as an internal development tool for a team who were building a game – and then the engineers realized that their collaboration tool was a better product than the game itself (Baer 2016). Other innovations are likely to be carefully planned. Understanding the nature of community, the value it brings to people, and the ways to support its growth may lead us to design the next form and the next business model.

We can choose business models that better incentivize the development of platforms that add to our individual and collective well-being (eudaimonia). If someone creates a new site that is like YouTube but everything is consistent with mainstream science, I'm going to switch to it. The choices you make as a consumer change what platforms become. I believe that there is pent-up demand for better-quality internet platforms, and you can do well by doing good. YouTube is just one example – this analysis applies to most internet sites and platforms. The profit motive alone does not magically make the right thing happen. Competition is needed – the best outcome for advancing both free speech and truth is to have lots of sites with competing standards, and let people decide which ones to frequent.

In neoliberal theory, healthy competition should solve all problems. I wonder if that could work, if there really was strong competition. Regardless, it's clear that it doesn't work when actual competition never emerges. Productive competition is not naturally emerging in our current economic system. Our current information space is dominated by a few huge players. We need public initiatives to foster the growth of healthy competition. Where that competition fails, some problems need to be changed with policy – passing laws that regulate what is not working.

New business models need to be *invented*. What do people value, and what are they willing to pay for? Targeted marketing is inextricably bound up with issues of privacy. Do people care about their privacy? Are people willing to pay more for privacy-preserving services? If so, then future entrepreneurs may invent new business models for privacy-conscious consumers. As of August 2020, the privacy-preserving search engine DuckDuckGo commands 0.5 percent of internet searches.[1] It will be interesting to see how their market share evolves over time, and whether more privacy-preserving options emerge for other types of software.

Each business model creates different incentives for the business and its users, and any business model can be leveraged in a more responsible or more exploitative way. The risk for users of some platforms is spending too much time or money there. This can damage the quality of people's lives. Analyzing in-game purchasing systems in video games, King et al. note that "Some in-game purchasing systems may represent financial hazards that contribute to player over-commitment to gaming activities and increase risk of negative financial and psychological consequences" (King et al. 2019, 141). Platforms can decide to encourage as much use as possible, or to encourage reasonable use. My hope is that designers will recognize the spectrum of outcomes, and design systems that encourage balanced expenditures of both time and money.

In an ideal world, internet entrepreneurs would naturally do well by doing good – that is, people who make

---

[1] https://gs.statcounter.com/search-engine-market-share

less-toxic sites that enrich participants' lives will also make more money. Currently, that's often not true. The intriguing question is whether we can invent new business models that align these goals more effortlessly.

Business models seem to drive our design decisions and are driving us in unhealthy directions. We have two options to remedy this. One is to invent new business models that drive us in better directions. The other is to bravely ignore the bottom line and take a more non-profit view – to put our values before our finances. I'm not sure if there really are magic business models that will make the internet a better place – that may be a naive hope. But one thing is certain: *More of the internet in the future should be non-profit.* A non-profit business model and worldview will let platforms put the needs of individuals and communities first.

There have been a variety of attempts at improving the internet through non-profit means. The most notable success is Mozilla, which builds open-source tools that embody their vision "to ensure the Internet is a global public resource, open and accessible to all. An Internet that truly puts people first, where individuals can shape their own experience and are empowered, safe and independent" (Mozilla n.d.). Under this umbrella, they have created the Firefox browser (which is more privacy-preserving than most other browsers), open-source audio tools, virtual-reality toolkits, and a host of other things. Part of why Mozilla has been so successful is because they have a business model which piggybacks off for-profit models. Every time someone does a search in the Firefox browser, the search engine used pays a small fee to Mozilla. They are funded by advertising indirectly, but in a way that doesn't change their basic values and mission.

Other attempts at non-profit civic spaces have taken a low-budget approach. For example, the free, open-source software (OSS) Mastodon provides an alternative to Twitter and the OSS project Mattermost provides an alternative to Slack. It's tremendously hard for tools like these to achieve wide public adoption, because they can't look or function like commercial sites built by teams of thousands of full-time designers and engineers. Most people have never heard of them, and wouldn't find them usable or appealing if they tried them. Public funding of non-profit social media efforts like these could enhance their value and give them a greater chance to win users and have impact. If we value social spaces that contribute to our civic well-being, then we need to publicly fund them as civic projects (like highways, railroads, and rural telephone and broadband access).

Although I do believe in the potential positive impact of open-source tools, they can still be misused. For example, the hate speech site Gab has adapted ("forked" in OSS terms) the software for Mastodon (Mastodon 2019). Tools are tools – a hammer can be used to build a house or to break windows. We need social and legal consequences for people who misuse them.

## Theoretical Summary

The business models that support socio-technical systems shape what those systems become. If we understand the impact of financial forces, then we can work to make finances *serve our larger goals*, rather than driving a system's design to unhealthy ends.

## Practical Implications

Markets shape online behavior in three notable ways. First, people's willingness to pay for access to a site filters who participates. Filters on who participates can reduce bad content and improve content quality, but also can work against equity if some people are financially excluded.

Second, the cost of managing online behavior shapes decisions about what is allowed, and the resources they have (both human and technical) to enforce the standards they envision. Perfect moderation is possible in theory if financial resources are unlimited. With realistic resources, platforms need to make hard choices. To a surprising degree, the cost of managing behavior shapes what online sites are viable.

Third, the way a site is financed changes the site's priorities. Sites that prioritize financial results over all other factors often end up promoting content that does not improve the lives of members or the state of the world. Instead, sites need to articulate values for what sort of world they want to help create.

# 8 How Can We Help the Internet to Bring Out the Best in Us All?

Since 2004, I've taught the required ethics class "Computing, Society, and Professionalism" to our undergraduates at Georgia Tech. We cover a variety of ethical theories, and then learn about issues of technology and society. We ask students to think about the ethical implications of the technologies we are creating.

My favorite ethical theory is virtue ethics. Virtue ethics traces its roots back to Aristotle, and suggests that the reason for doing good is to be a good person. If you embody the virtues that you value, you can reach toward a state of "eudaimonia." Eudaimonia is hard to translate from Greek, but roughly means "the kind of happiness that is worth having."

Virtue ethics argues that being virtuous is not a binary state – it is something you must continually strive for. Other ethical theories are often used to provide an answer to a dilemma – what is the right thing to do in this situation? Virtue ethics suggests that if you value honesty, cultivating your qualities of honesty is a lifelong pursuit (Stanford Encyclopedia of Philosophy 2016).

I believe we need a virtue ethics for designers and users of the internet. Communications technologies are reshaping our society and our world. As we create those technologies, we must ask: What kind of world do we hope to create? *What are our goals for society*

213

*(our virtues), and how can we help cultivate them with the ways we communicate?*

In this conclusion, I'll revisit each of the topics I discussed in previous chapters with this lens: How can we leverage that design feature to help the internet bring out the best in us all?

## Community

In Chapter 1, I explored how the internet helps us to form communities. Some forms of community (like church groups or parent–teacher associations) have a long history, and others have been made possible by internet technology. For any group we can ask, what value does it bring to its members? In what ways do people support one another, and how could that be enhanced? We can accomplish that by improving existing groups or imagining new ones.

I don't believe all the possible kinds of community have been invented yet. Over the course of my life, I have found different online groups that have each served as my "third place" for a time. In the 1990s, I spent some time on a Star Trek-themed text-based role-playing game. I pretended to be a Starfleet diplomat, and became friends with a Ferengi ship captain (actually an engineer at Ford Motor Company in Detroit).

In the mid-2000s, I spent time discussing food allergies with other parents on the kids with food allergies bulletin board. They gave me critical safety advice, egg- and dairy-free recipes, and supportive friends who would listen, whatever the challenge or stress I faced. My friends there understood my challenges on both a practical and emotional level.

Today, I hang out with a group of moderators of a subreddit on our mod team's Slack. Sometimes we talk about content moderation decisions for our subreddit, but we also share political news, discuss the latest movies and television, and share pictures of food we have cooked. The design of Slack lets us have channels for serious conversations about our shared volunteer work, and a myriad of channels on other topics – like one for memes, one for parenting, and one for politics. The theme of the subreddit brought us together, and means we share values and a view of the world. When I travel, the first question I ask myself is "Is there someone from our mod team in that area who I could meet for coffee?"

When I compare these three communities, it strikes me that the quality of interaction has improved over time. I had nothing much in common with my fellow role-players except being fans of Star Trek. Liking the same television show did give us a shared sensibility. I had a lot in common with the allergy parents – we were going through the same stressful phase of life scrutinizing food labels and packing epi-pens everywhere, and my understanding of the art and science of living with food allergies deepened through my interaction with them. I have the most in common with my current friends on my subreddit's Slack. We share values, and I find them smart and interesting. I can rely on them to share links with me that enrich my worldview about all sorts of topics, and have nuanced discussions about what is going on in the world.

A successful online group becomes the people you turn to, like the bereaved grandmother from Chapter 1 who turned to the Mini Cooper brand community when she needed support for devastating news in the middle of the night.

The quality of interaction I have experienced in these groups has improved from the 1990s to now. It's partly of course that I've matured. But so has the technology. There are design features of Slack that support more complex and nuanced interaction than the ASCII connection over Telnet that ran my Star Trek role-playing game. There are also forms of group interaction that we now understand better.

If you are a member of an online community, you have impact in the example you set for others. This is particularly true if you are a "regular" of a group. As we saw in Chapter 1, the regulars set the tone for the behavior of the group. Ask yourself, how can we make this place supportive and help it to better fulfill its potential? Online groups create social worlds. Each of us co-creates those worlds in how kind, understanding, and patient we are with one another, and in the standards we set for ourselves and others.

If you are a designer of an online social platform, ask yourself what kind of world this site is helping to create. Your driving consideration should be thinking hard about how to improve people's lives, individually and collectively. How can the site help the emergence of knowledge (which, as we saw in Chapter 3, is justified, true belief)? How can it be a supportive third place? These questions should be primary. Unfortunately, what actually happens in reality today is that "how to make the most possible money" tends to drive design. As I'll argue below, I believe that to enhance the value the internet brings, we need to rethink business models that support it. We need more forums on the internet that are non-profit, driven by goals for their members and not by the financial bottom line.

## Collaboration

In Chapter 2 I explored the impressive things that people contributing content together can accomplish. As an internet user, I encourage you to find the places that need you. It's tremendously satisfying to see something you created that others find useful. It might be correcting a Wikipedia page, sharing a how-to video, or a cute picture of your cat. Helping create content that enlightens, amuses, or helps others accomplish something is both rewarding for you and a service for them.

For designers of online sites, I challenge you to find new ways to empower people to contribute content constructively. We still have oceans of untapped human potential. If everyone took the least fulfilling and useful half-hour of their day and devoted it to building a shared resource, think what we could accomplish. Different kinds of people need different kinds of opportunities to contribute. Good tools and social support for their use make new kinds of collaborative content creation possible.

## Truth and Knowledge

In Chapters 3 and 4, I explored the basic nature of truth and knowledge, and how groups of people on the internet engage in the social construction of knowledge. In a profound sense, what we all agree is true is what is literally true – at least for now. What we collectively agree is true matters.

At the time I am writing in 2020, we have a crisis of fake information online. This crisis is about to get worse. Artificial intelligence tools like GPT-3 (Brown et al. 2020) can now create compelling fake text, and "deep fake" technology can create videos that are tough to distinguish from real recordings (Kietzmann et al. 2019). These technologies are continually improving, and telling real content from AI-generated content is going to become impossible even for the most savvy human.

One way to address these problems is to fight AI with AI: Create programs that annotate online information with metrics of reliability and accounts of the information's provenance. We will need mixed-initiative approaches that combine human intelligence with machine. The challenge is that those tools don't work particularly well yet.

Recently I saw a comically wrong "fact check" on Facebook.[1] The original post showed a picture of actress Diana Rigg (who had just passed away) in one of her first films, and a picture of her in the HBO television series *Game of Thrones*. The poster commented that she hadn't realized these were the same person. The post was correct – Diana Rigg played Olenna Tyrell in *Game of Thrones*. The fact check noted that this was false because it was not actually a photo of "Delhi CM Arvind Kejriwal" (who looks nothing like Rigg). This is puzzling. Presumably some kind of

---

[1] Thanks to Sue Dynarski for posting the weird fact check.

algorithmic error is behind the mistake. Services that do automatic fact-checking are far from working correctly. It is possible that making them work well will require changes throughout the software pipeline, starting with embedding data when content is first generated, and noting each modification through the pipeline.

Even if fact-checking services improve dramatically in quality, they will still be vulnerable to deliberate undermining. It's often easier to correct accidental misinformation than deliberate disinformation. There is a growing epidemic of state-sponsored disinformation, much of which is designed to manipulate public opinion. Russian "troll farms" have been working over the last several years to increase divisiveness in the United States, though it's unclear how much impact they have had (Bail et al. 2020; Starbird et al. 2019). We can find ways to detect and block that content, but then their methods will become more sophisticated. We will likely be trapped in this information "arms race" indefinitely.

While it's challenging to counter disinformation from unofficial sources, it's near impossible to counter when it comes from sanctioned, official sources. For example, the United States was unprepared to respond to the challenge of Donald Trump's false claims that he won the 2020 presidential election. Writing this in January 2021, it seems likely that the false information he spread may have a long half-life. Social media played a role in spreading dangerous false information and giving it credibility. This is not the first time a supposedly credible figure has led a significant disinformation campaign, and it is unlikely to be the last. We are increasingly vulnerable to cynical manipulation of our information landscape, and need to rethink our safeguards. I hope people like readers of this book can help.

As users of the internet, we need to continually increase our skepticism about all information we receive over the coming years. If you have the financial means, invest in for-pay platforms and reliability services that help you to not get misled by false content. I am worried that "truth" is going to increasingly become a privilege of the rich as we drift toward an information space where free information sources are less reliable than those you pay for. One solution is to invest more public funding in supporting high-quality information sources (for example, like the Corporation for Public Broadcasting). Furthermore, information literacy skills need more emphasis throughout our education system and public discourse. Nothing about this is easy. It took all of Chapter 3 of this book to explain that the answer to the question "Should you believe Wikipedia?" is "It depends on the popularity of the page." We all need more education in both underlying principles and practical strategies for judging the quality of information.

Should users of the internet simply avoid spreading false content, or should they also work to correct it? Currently there's often no easy way to do so. As we saw in the discussion of the redesign of Yahoo Answers in Chapter 7, empowering users to flag bad content can work surprisingly well. Designers of sites can make it possible for users to help.

For creators of sites where people share information, it is your ethical responsibility to do everything in your power to make it easier for your members to make reasonable judgments about what to believe. Your goal is not to tell people what to believe, but to give people sufficient metadata to help them to make smart choices about what to believe. This can't be an after-thought in your platform's design – it needs to be a primary focus.

## Identity

In Chapter 5 I talked about identity – all the ways we present ourselves online, and how that shapes online interaction. As a user of the internet, it's important to reflect on how you present yourself in different contexts, and how that shapes how people react to you. How you present yourself can shape how the group behaves as a whole. It's also important to be aware of your privacy, and the potential impact of information about yourself that you reveal.

If you are a researcher, I have a grand challenge to propose. I believe there is room for fundamental improvement in the ways we represent online identity. Problems with online identity today include the following:

- It's too hard to tell who is a child. It should be possible to have sites with adult content that are restricted to adults, and sites for children that are just for children.
- It's possible for different people to claim to be the same person.
- It's too hard to block trolls and others who repeatedly break rules. If a site owner blocks someone, the miscreant often can come back with a new account – again and again.

I can imagine a system of "identity servers." To sign up for an account on a social network, the network might require that you have an account with a particular identity verification service. The service would be run by an independent third party, and would charge a small fee for hosting your identity. They would verify some part of your identity (maybe your legal name, or perhaps just your age), and then delete the data you provided but maintain a secure identity record. Cryptography would help keep your identity secure. Going forward, the service could answer questions like "yes, this person is verified to be an adult" or "yes, this person is the same one who sent that message last week," but have no other information about who the person might be.

Regarding trolls returning over and over, the system probably couldn't prevent someone from creating a new identity account. However, the need to create a new account on the identity service creates a bit of design friction. As we saw in Chapter 7, on the Something Awful Forums you need to pay a small fee for a new account if you are banned (Pater et al. 2014). This small barrier dramatically changes people's behavior. Similarly, the need to create a new identity account and pay a small fee might not discourage banned trolls from coming back a few times, but would discourage them from coming back hundreds of times.

There are major challenges to implementing something like this. The biggest concern is that you would need to trust the identity service, and there would be huge problems if a service was mismanaged or hacked. It's important to note that being identified can be a great risk for minorities, members of marginalized groups, and people living under oppressive regimes. It's an intriguing question to think about secure designs where the system can't hand over compromising information even under threat of force, because it doesn't have it.

My proposal here is just a half-baked sketch, but I hope a research team will take on the challenge. The broader point is: We don't think about the basic design of online identity enough. I believe a better system is possible.

## Living with and Managing Bad Behavior

Chapters 6 and 7 focused on managing bad behavior. An old cliché says that if you lie down with dogs, you wake up with fleas. My advice for users of the internet at the current moment in history is: *Be mindful about what platforms you use.* Think hard about the impact a particular platform or media source is having on you and on the world, and make deliberate choices when you can.

Suppose a platform is surrounding you with accidental misinformation or deliberate disinformation. Or perhaps the platform is a conduit for hate speech or a vector for harassment. As we saw in the work of Albert Hirschman, your two main options are *voice* and *exit*. You can advocate for change within the platform (voice), or find a different place to get your information and spend your time (exit).

When you exercise your right to exit, you communicate a message to the platform. They may work harder to improve things if enough people leave. If you do leave, you might check back again in months or years to see if they've improved. Platforms are trying to improve in this area, and they may even be successful.

An important third option on many sites is to found your own subgroup. On Facebook you can easily start a new Facebook group. On Reddit, you can easily start a new subreddit. Then you are in charge, and can try to make the group live up to your standards and aspirations.

If you design or manage an online site, I wish you good luck. These problems are hard. We are going to need big improvements in both AI technology to assist with content moderation, and major shifts in national and international policy to address the festering problems of false and offensive content on the internet. Unfortunately, I don't believe these problems will ever be "solved" to anyone's satisfaction. It's an eternal arms race between defensive and offensive technologies, between good actors and bad.

How to address these issues should be primary in your design process. It won't work if you start considering misuse as an after-thought. My former PhD student Casey Fiesler and her student Natalie Garrett have coined the term "ethical debt." Developers commonly talk about "technical debt." If you leave a technical problem to be dealt with later, the time needed to address it goes up. Ethical concerns are similar. We need to do a better job of anticipating ethical issues raised by our communications technologies (Fiesler and Garrett 2020). Managing bad behavior is a prime example. Waiting to see what bad things happen after a system is live used to be a workable strategy for online sites, but that time is past. Managing bad content and bad behavior need to be considerations from the start of a design process.

For researchers, issues of managing wrong information and abusive behavior online provide a fascinating set of problems to work on. Further, addressing those problems is an opportunity to have a positive impact on the world.

Chapter 7 also highlights ways that the financial model that supports a site ends up driving the site's design. Business models shape what kinds of sites are viable. Right now, those models are driving us toward some dysfunctional outcomes like sites that make money off spreading conspiracy theories and hate speech. Business models to support internet platforms and services are still being invented. Innovation in business models is a potential catalyst for positive change. However, more fundamentally, we need more sites that are non-profit and whose design is driven by trying to enhance quality of life for individuals and societies.

## The Need for an Educated Citizenry

In April 2018, Facebook founder and CEO Mark Zuckerberg was called to testify before the US Congress to respond to allegations of misuse of user data by the site and its partner Cambridge Analytica. Reporter Emily Stewart wrote after the hearings that "Senators seem to agree they want to fix something about Facebook. They have no idea what" (Stewart 2018). During the hearings, several Members of Congress displayed a basic lack of understanding of what Facebook is and how it works. Senator Lindsey Graham asked Zuckerberg, "Is Twitter the same as what you do?" Senator Orrin Hatch asked, "How do you sustain a business model in which users don't pay for your service?" (Zuckerberg politely told him that they sell ads) (Zetlin 2018). Our policy-makers can't guide the future of the internet if they don't understand it. Having national leaders who don't understand the basics of the internet is a poignant illustration. More broadly, this lack of knowledge is a problem at all levels of society. Better outcomes depend not just on policy-makers and high-tech developers, but on all of us as informed citizens and smart consumers.

The future of the internet will be shaped by people's basic internet and information literacy. Researcher danah boyd points out that "media literacy" education is already taught in schools, but in a form that is not really helping much (boyd 2018). Curricula about the nature of information need to be much more extensive, and integrated throughout schooling – not something you do for one week in fourth grade. We also need to educate ourselves, and to expect our elected representatives to be information-literate.

Throughout this book, I've tried to provide accessible summaries of theoretical readings. The goal is to give you a basic understanding and to encourage you to read the originals. Understanding the internet is a new field that is evolving. We all need a more nuanced understanding, and theory can help. This is not just for high-tech designers, but for everyone – there are few professions untouched by this technology. What do you wish members of the US Congress had known before questioning Zuckerberg? We all need to learn those ideas, and to make sure they are widely taught.

## Aspiration and Design

I look back at the *World Book Encyclopedia* that is still in my childhood bedroom, that my mother saved to buy, and am astonished – how far we have come! It's hard for me to explain to my children how we used to do things, back when you couldn't just do an online search and get the answer to almost anything.

At the same time, we as a society can do better at a host of things – like taking better care of the environment, being pro-active about public health, treating everyone in our society fairly, fighting racism, and lessening economic inequality. As the internet reshapes every aspect of our society, we must ask the question: What kind of world do we want to live in? Our communications technologies shape that world. How can technologists help?

In 2018, the Association for Computing Machinery (ACM) rewrote its code of ethics for the first time in twenty-five years. I participated in one three-day meeting where we rewrote parts of the code, and it was the greatest privilege of my career. The code has a series of ethical imperatives. Thinking about the bigger picture, this one stands out:

> 3.7 Recognize and take special care of systems that become integrated into the infrastructure of society.
>
> Even the simplest computer systems have the potential to impact all aspects of society when integrated with everyday activities such as commerce, travel, government, healthcare, and education. When organizations and groups develop systems that become

an important part of the infrastructure of society, their leaders have an added responsibility to be good stewards of these systems. Part of that stewardship requires establishing policies for fair system access, including for those who may have been excluded. That stewardship also requires that computing professionals monitor the level of integration of their systems into the infrastructure of society. As the level of adoption changes, the ethical responsibilities of the organization or group are likely to change as well. Continual monitoring of how society is using a system will allow the organization or group to remain consistent with their ethical obligations outlined in the Code. When appropriate standards of care do not exist, computing professionals have a duty to ensure they are developed. (ACM 2018)

Much of the internet has become integrated into the infrastructure of society in ways that give us new ethical obligations. Although earlier in this chapter I suggested you might choose not to use platforms that bring you false information or harassment, in some cases that's simply not possible. You might be required to use a platform for your job. Or an organization might have to use a platform for outreach because that's where the people are. For example, in her dissertation research, my former PhD student Sucheta Ghoshal found that many grassroots groups would prefer not to use Facebook because it excludes economically less-advantaged members who don't have a smartphone or computer. However, so many people are on Facebook that they end up doing outreach on the platform anyway (Ghoshal and Bruckman 2019). Platforms that people can't choose not to use have added ethical responsibilities to society as a whole.

We need to identify our values before we start creating new pieces of technology or modifying old ones. In their conceptualization of "value-sensitive design," Friedman et al. propose that designers do the following:

- "Start with a value, technology, or context of use."
- "Identify direct and indirect stakeholders."
- "Identify benefits and harms of each stakeholder group."
- "Map benefits and harms onto corresponding values."
- "Conduct a conceptual investigation of key values."
- "Identify potential value conflicts."
- "Integrate value considerations into one's organizational structure." (Friedman et al. 2006)

That's a high bar, but it's worth working toward. In truth, all design is value-centered design. Technology is never neutral. The only question is whether we are paying attention to what our implicit values are, and deliberately trying to have a positive impact on the world or not.

Design features of online communities shape human behavior. We can leverage those features to encourage more thoughtful discussions, greater mutual understanding, and the growth of knowledge.

If you are a designer of information and communications technologies, throughout this book I've tried to give you some tools to help you reflect on your design choices. The choices you make shape what sort of human behavior emerges as a result. If you are a participant in online communication, think hard about what platforms you choose to use, and use your voice to ask that platforms provide a better experience for everyone. Our communications technologies shape who we are as individuals, communities, and societies. Understanding them better can empower us to work toward better outcomes.

# REFERENCES

ACM. 2018. "ACM code of ethics and professional conduct."
https://ethics.acm.org

Adler, Paul, and Seok-Woo Kwon. 2002. "Social Capital: Prospects
for a New Concept." *Academy of Management Review* 27 (1):
17–40. https://doi.org/10.5465/amr.2002.5922314

Ammari, Tawfiq, Sarita Schoenebeck, and Daniel M. Romero.
2019. "Self-declared Throwaway Accounts on Reddit: How
Platform Affordances and Shared Norms Enable Parenting
Disclosure and Support." *Proceedings of the ACM on Human-
Computer Interaction, CSCW.* https://doi.org/10.1145/3359237

Appel, Lora, Punit Dadlani, Maria Dwyer, et al. 2014. "Testing the
validity of social capital measures in the study of information
and communication technologies." *Information,
Communication & Society* 17 (4): 398–416. https://doi.org/10
.1080/1369118X.2014.884612

Atkinson, Nancy. 2009. "Galaxy Zoo is expanding to include a
whole new 'Zooniverse'." *Universe Today.* www.universetoday
.com/47501/galaxy-zoo-is-expanding-to-include-a-whole-new-
zooniverse

Baase, Sara. 2013. *Gift of Fire.* 4th ed. Harlow: Pearson.

Baer, Drake. 2016. "Inside the video game roots of Slack, everyone's
favorite workplace messaging app." *Business Insider.* www
.businessinsider.com/inside-the-video-game-roots-of-slack-2016-3

Bail, Christopher, Brian Guay, Emily Maloney, et al. 2020.
"Assessing the Russian Internet Research Agency's impact on
the political attitudes and behaviors of American Twitter users in
late 2017." *Proceedings of the National Academy of Sciences*
117 (1). https://doi.org/10.1073/pnas.1906420116

Bao, Patti, Brent Hecht, Samuel Carton, et al. 2012. "Omnipedia: bridging the Wikipedia language gap." *Proceedings of the 2012 ACM Annual Conference on Human Factors in Computing Systems – CHI '12.* https://doi.org/10.1145/2207676.2208553

Baron, Naomi S. 2004. "See you online: gender issues in college student use of instant messaging." *Journal of Language and Social Psychology* 23: 397–423. https://doi.org/10.1177/0261927X04269585

Bartle, Richard. 1996. "Hearts, diamonds, clubs, spades: players who suit MUDs." *Journal of MUD Research* 1 (1).

Baum, Dan. 2005. "Battle lessons: what the generals don't know." *The New Yorker*: 42–48. www.newyorker.com/magazine/2005/01/17/battle-lessons

Baym, Nancy. 2010. *Personal Connections in the Digital Age.* Cambridge: Polity Press.

BBC. 2020. "Coronavirus: YouTube bans 'medically unsubstantiated' content." www.bbc.com/news/technology-52388586

Becker, Howard. 1952. "Social-class variations in the teacher–pupil relationship." *Journal of Educational Sociology* 25 (8): 451–465. https://doi.org/https://doi.org/10.2307/2263957

Becker, Rachel. 2019. "Facebook outlines plans to curb anti-vax conspiracy theories." *The Verge.* www.theverge.com/2019/3/7/18255107/facebook-anti-vaccine-misinformation-measles-outbreaks-group-page-recommendations-removal

Benkler, Yochai. 2002. "Coase's penguin, or, Linux and the nature of the firm." *Yale Law Journal* 112 (3): 369–446. https://doi.org/10.2307/1562247

Berman, Joshua, and Amy Bruckman. 2001. "The Turing game: exploring identity in an online environment." *Convergence* 7 (3): 83–102. https://doi.org/10.1177/135485650100700307

Bernstein, Michael S., Andrés Monroy-Hernández, Drew Harry, et al. 2011. "4chan and /b/: an analysis of anonymity and ephemerality in a large online community." *Proceedings of the International AAAI Conference on Web and Social Media.* https://ojs.aaai.org/index.php/ICWSM/article/view/14134

Borges, Jorge Luis, and Andrew Hurley. 1999. *Collected Fictions.* New York: Penguin.

boyd, danah. 2011. "'Real names' policies are an abuse of power." www.zephoria.org/thoughts/archives/2011/08/04/real-names .html

boyd, danah. 2018. "You think you want media literacy . . . do you?" https://points.datasociety.net/you-think-you-want-media-literacy-do-you-7cad6af18ec2

Brock, André. 2012. "From the blackhand side: Twitter as a cultural conversation." *Journal of Broadcasting and Electronic Media* 56 (4): 529–549. https://doi.org/10.1080/08838151.2012 .732147

Brock, André. 2020. *Distributed Blackness: African American Cybercultures.* New York: NYU Press.

Brown, Tom B., Benjamin Mann, Nick Ryder, et al. 2020. "Language models are few-shot learners." https://arxiv.org/abs/ 2005.14165

Bruckman, A. 1996. "Finding one's own space in cyberspace." *Technology Review* 99 (1): 48–54. www.cc.gatech.edu/~asb/ papers/tr-finding-ones-own.pdf

Bruckman, A. 2006. "'A new perspective on community' and its implications for computer-mediated communication systems." *CHI '06 Extended Abstracts on Human Factors in Computing Systems.* https://doi.org/10.1145/1125451.1125579

Bruckman, A. 2010. "Amy's prediction: in 20 years no one will be qualified to be president." https://nextbison.wordpress.com/ 2010/01/22/amys-prediction-in-20-years-no-one-will-be-qualified-to-be-president

Bruckman, A., and M. Resnick. 1995. "The MediaMOO Project: constructionism and professional community." *Convergence:*

*The International Journal of Research into New Media Technologies* 1 (1). https://doi.org/10.1177/135485659500100110

Bruckman, A., P. Curtis, C. Figallo, and B. Laurel. 1994. "Approaches to managing deviant behavior in virtual communities." *CHI '94: Conference Companion on Human Factors in Computing Systems.* https://doi.org/10.1145/259963.260231

Bruckman, A., C. Danis, C. Lampe, J. Sternberg, and C. Waldron. 2006. "Managing deviant behavior in online communities." *CHI '06 Extended Abstracts on Human Factors in Computing Systems.* https://doi.org/10.1145/1125451.1125458

Bryant, Susan, Andrea Forte, and Amy Bruckman. 2005. "Becoming Wikipedian: transformation of participation in an collaborative online encyclopedia." *GROUP '05: Proceedings of the 2005 International ACM SIGGROUP Conference on Supporting Group Work.* https://doi.org/10.1145/1099203.1099205

Buni, Catherine, and Soraya Chemaly. 2016. "The secret rules of the internet." *The Verge.* www.theverge.com/2016/4/13/11387934/internet-moderator-history-youtube-facebook-reddit-censorship-free-speech

Burt, Ronald S. 2004. "Structural holes and good ideas." American *Journal of Sociology* 110 (2): 349–399. https://doi.org/10.1086/421787

Chancellor, Stevie, Jessica Pater, Trustin Clear, Eric Gilbert, and Munmun De Choudhury. 2016. "#thyghgapp: Instagram content moderation and lexical variation in pro-eating disorder communities." *CSCW '16: Proceedings of the 19th ACM Conference on Computer-Supported Cooperative Work & Social Computing.* https://doi.org/10.1145/2818048.2819963

Chandrasekharan, Eshwar, Umashanthi Pavalanathan, Anirudh Srinivasan, et al. 2017. "You Can't Stay Here: The Efficacy of Reddit's 2015 Ban Examined through Hate Speech." *Proceedings of the ACM on Human–Computer Interaction* 1 (CSCW): 1–22. https://doi.org/10.1145/3134666

Chandrasekharan, E., M. Samory, S. Jhaver, et al. 2018. "The Internet's hidden rules: an empirical study of Reddit norm violations at micro, meso, and macro scales." *Proceedings of the ACM on Human-Computer Interaction 2 (CSCW).* https://doi .org/10.1145/3274301

Chappell, Bill. 2016. "Boaty by another name: 'Sir David Attenborough' is chosen for British research ship." National Public Radio. www.npr.org/sections/thetwo-way/2016/05/06/ 477010650/boaty-by-another-name-sir-david-attenborough-is-chosen-for-british-research-ship

Chesney, Robert, and Danielle Keats Citron. 2018. "Deep Fakes: A Looming Challenge for Privacy, Democracy, and National Security." *SSRN Electronic Journal.* https://doi.org/10.2139/ssrn .3213954

Citron, Danielle. 2014. *Hate Crimes in Cyberspace.* Cambridge, MA: Harvard University Press.

Clark, David D. 2018. *Designing an Internet.* Cambridge, MA: MIT Press.

Coleman, Gabriella. 2014. *Hacker, Hoaxer, Whistleblower, Spy.* London: Verso.

Collins, Allan, John Seely Brown, and Susan E. Newman. 1989. "Cognitive apprenticeship: teaching the crafts of reading, writing, and mathematics." In L. B. Resnick (ed.), *Knowing, Learning, and Instruction: Essays in Honor of Robert Glaser,* 453–494. Hillsdale, NJ: Lawrence Erlbaum Associates.

Cooper, Seth, Firas Khatib, Adrien Treuille, et al. 2010. "Predicting protein structures with a multiplayer online game." *Nature* 466 (7307): 756–760. https://doi.org/10.1038/nature09304

Cornell Lab of Ornithology. n.d. "NestWatch." https://nestwatch.org

Cranshaw, Justin, and Aniket Kittur. 2011. "The polymath project: lessons from a successful online collaboration in mathematics."

*Proceedings of the 2011 Annual Conference on Computer Human Interaction*. https://doi.org/10.1145/1978942.1979213

Crowston, Kevin, Kangning Wei, James Howison, and Andrea Wiggins. 2012. "Free/Libre open-source software development." *ACM Computing Surveys* 44 (2): 1–35. https://doi.org/10.1145/2089125.2089127

De Choudhury, Munmun, Shagun Jhaver, Benjamin Sugar, and Ingmar Weber. 2016. "Social Media Participation in an Activist Movement for Racial Equality." *Proceedings of the 10th International Conference on Web and Social Media, ICWSM 2016*. https://ojs.aaai.org/index.php/ICWSM/article/view/14758

de Saussure, Ferdinand. 1959. *Course in General Linguistics*. New York: McGraw-Hill.

Dibbell, Julian. 1993. "A rape in cyberspace." *The Village Voice*: 36–42.

Dix, Alan, Janet Finlay, Gregory Abowd, and Russell Beale. 1998. *Human–Computer Interaction*. Hoboken, NJ: Prentice Hall.

Domroese, Margret C., and Elizabeth A. Johnson. 2017. "Why watch bees? Motivations of citizen science volunteers in the Great Pollinator Project." *Biological Conservation* 208: 40–47. https://doi.org/10.1016/J.BIOCON.2016.08.020

Donath, Judith. 2002. "Identity and deception in the virtual community." In Peter Kollock and Marc Smith (eds.), *Communities in Cyberspace*. London: Taylor and Francis.

Donath, Judith. 2014. "We need online alter egos now more than ever." *Wired*. www.wired.com/2014/04/why-we-need-online-alter-egos-now-more-than-ever

Dwyer, Colin. 2017. "Boaty McBoatface Makes Its Triumphant Return, Hauling 'Unprecedented Data'." National Public Radio. www.npr.org/sections/thetwo-way/2017/06/28/534744971/boaty-mcboatface-makes-its-triumphant-return-hauling-unprecedented-data

Ellison, Nicole B., Charles Steinfield, and Cliff Lampe. 2007. "The Benefits of Facebook 'Friends': Social Capital and College

Students' Use of Online Social Network Sites" *Journal of Computer-Mediated Communication* 12 (4): 1143–1168. https://doi.org/10.1111/j.1083-6101.2007.00367.x

Facebook. 2015. "Community Support FYI: Improving the Names Process on Facebook." https://newsroom.fb.com/news/2015/12/community-support-fyi-improving-the-names-process-on-facebook

Fallis, Don. 2008. "Towards an epistemology of Wikipedia." *Journal of the American Society for Information Science and Technology* 589 (10): 1662–1674. https://doi.org/10.1002/asi.20870

Farmer, Randy, and Bryce Glass. 2010. "Case study: Yahoo! Answers community content moderation." In *Building Web Reputation Systems*, chapter 10. Sebastopol, CA: O'Reilly Press.

Feldman, Richard. 2003. *Epistemology*. Hoboken, NJ: Prentice Hall.

Field, Jonathan Beecher. 2019. *Town Hall Meetings and the Death of Deliberation*. Minneapolis, MN: University of Minnesota Press.

Fiesler, Casey. 2007. "Imagined identities: Harry Potter, roleplaying, and blogs." In L. Hilman (ed.), *The Witching Hour: A Magical Compendium*, 147–148. Bloomington, IN: Xlibris Corporation.

Fiesler, Casey, and Amy Bruckman. 2019. "Creativity, Copyright, and Close-Knit Communities: A Case Study of Online Social Norm Formation and Enforcement Online." *Proceedings of the ACM on Human-Computer Interaction 3 (GROUP)*. https://doi.org/10.1145/3361122

Fiesler, Casey, and Natalie Garrett. 2020. "Ethical tech starts with addressing ethical debt." *Wired*. www.wired.com/story/opinion-ethical-tech-starts-with-addressing-ethical-debt

Fiesler, Casey, Cliff Lampe, and Amy Bruckman. 2016. "Reality and Perception of Copyright Terms of Service for Online

Content Creation." *CSCW '16: Proceedings of the 19th ACM Conference on Computer-Supported Cooperative Work & Social Computing (CSCW)*. https://doi.org/10.1145/2818048.2819931

Florini, Sarah. 2014. "Tweets, Tweeps, and Signifyin': Communication and Cultural Performance on 'Black Twitter'." *Television and New Media* 15 (3): 223–237. https://doi.org/10.1177/1527476413480247

Fox, Annie B., Danuta Bukatko, Mark Hallahan, and Mary Crawford. 2007. "The Medium Makes the Difference: Gender Similarities and Differences in Instant Messaging." *Journal of Language and Social Psychology* 26 (4): 389–397. https://doi.org/10.1177/0261927X07306982

Friedman, Batya, Peter H. Kahn, and Alan Borning. 2006. "Value-sensitive design and information systems." In Ping Zhang and Dennis Galletta (eds.), *Human–Computer Interaction and Management Information Systems: Applications*, 348–372. New York: M. E. Sharpe.

Frost-Arnold, Karen. 2018. "Wikipedia." In David Coady and James Chase (eds.), *The Routledge Handbook of Applied Epistemology*, chapter 3. London: Routledge.

FTC. 2020. "Complying with COPPA: frequently asked questions." www.ftc.gov/tips-advice/business-center/guidance/complying-coppa-frequently-asked-questions-0

Garfinkel, Simson. 2000. *Database Nation*. Sebastopol, CA: O'Reilly Press.

Garwood, Christine. 2007. *Flat Earth: The History of an Infamous Idea*. New York: Thomas Dunne Books.

Geiger, R. Stuart, and Aaron Halfaker. 2013. "When the levee breaks: without bots, what happens to Wikipedia's quality control processes?" *Proceedings of the 9th International Symposium on Open Collaboration – WikiSym '13*. https://doi.org/10.1145/2491055.2491061

Geiger, R. Stuart, and David Ribes. 2010. "The work of sustaining order in Wikipedia." *CSCW '10: Proceedings of the 2010 ACM Conference on Computer Supported Cooperative Work (CSCW)*. https://doi.org/10.1145/1718918.1718941

Ghoshal, Sucheta, and Amy Bruckman. 2019. "The Role of Social Computing Technologies in Grassroots Movement Building." *ACM Transactions on Computer–Human Interaction* 26 (3). https://doi.org/10.1145/3318140

Gillespie, Tarleton. 2018. *Custodians of the Internet: Platforms, Content Moderation, and the Hidden Decisions That Shape Social Media.* New York: NYU Press.

Gleave, Eric, Howard T. Welser, Thomas M. Lento, and Marc A. Smith. 2009. "A conceptual and operational definition of 'social role' in online community." *42nd Annual Hawaii International Conference on System Sciences (HICSS)*. https://doi.org/10.1109/HICSS.2009.6

Goffman, Erving. 1959. *The Presentation of Self in Everyday Life.* New York: Doubleday.

Goldman, Alvin I. 1999. *Knowledge in a Social World.* Oxford: Oxford University Press.

Gonzales, Joseph A., Casey Fiesler, and Amy Bruckman. 2015. "Towards an Appropriable CSCW Tool Ecology." *Proceedings of the 18th ACM Conference on Computer Supported Cooperative Work & Social Computing (CSCW).* https://doi.org/10.1145/2675133.2675240

Gotterbarn, Don, Amy Bruckman, Catherine Flick, Keith Miller, and Marty Wolf. 2018. "ACM code of ethics: a guide for positive action." *Communications of the ACM* 61 (1): 121–128. http://dx.doi.org/10.1145/3173016

Granovetter, Mark S. 1973. "The Strength of Weak Ties." *American Journal of Sociology* 78 (6): 1360–1380. https://doi.org/10.1086/225469

Greco, John. 2021. *The Transmission of Knowledge*. Cambridge: Cambridge University Press.

Grimmelmann, James. 2006. "Regulation by Software." *Yale Law Journal* 114: 1719–1758. https://heinonline.org/HOL/P?h=hein .journals/ylr114&i=1738

Halavais, Alexander, and Derek Lackaff. 2008. "An Analysis of Topical Coverage of Wikipedia." *Journal of Computer-Mediated Communication* 13 (2): 429–440. https://doi.org/10 .1111/j.1083-6101.2008.00403.x

Hamblin, T. J. 1981. "Fake!" *British Medical Journal* 283 (6307): 1671. https://dx.doi.org/10.1136%2Fbmj.283.6307.1671

Hampton, Keith. 2016. "Persistent and Pervasive Community: New Communication Technologies and the Future of Community." *American Behavioral Scientist* 60 (1): 101–124. https://doi.org/10.1177/0002764215601714

Hampton, Keith, and Barry Wellman. 2018. "Lost and Saved . . . Again: The Moral Panic about the Loss of Community Takes Hold of Social Media." *Contemporary Sociology* 47 (6): 643–651. https://doi.org/10.1177/0094306118805415

Hampton, Keith, Chul-joo Lee, and Eun Ja Her. 2011. "How new media affords network diversity: direct and mediated access to social capital through participation in local social settings." *New Media & Society* 13 (7): 1031–1049. https://doi.org/10.1177% 2F1461444810390342

Hampton, Keith, Lee Rainie, Weixu Lu, Inyoung Shin, and Kristen Purcell. 2014. "Social Media and the Spiral of Silence." Pew Research Center. www.pewresearch.org/internet/2014/08/26/ social-media-and-the-spiral-of-silence

Hampton, Keith, Lee Rainie, Weixu Lu, Inyoung Shin, and Kristen Purcell. 2015. "Social Media and the Cost of Caring." Pew Research Center. www.pewinternet.org/2015/01/15/social-media-and-stress

Haywood, Benjamin Kent. 2014. "Birds and Beaches: The Affective Geographies and Sense of Place of Participants in the COASST

Citizen Science Program." ProQuest Dissertations and Theses. https://scholarcommons.sc.edu/etd/2748/

Heersmink, Richard. 2017. "A Virtue Epistemology of the Internet: Search Engines, Intellectual Virtues, and Education." *Social Epistemology* 32 (1): 1–12. https://doi.org/10.1080/02691728.2017 .1383530

Hirschman, Albert. 1970. *Exit, Voice, and Loyalty.* Cambridge, MA: Harvard University Press.

Hoffman, Judy, Eric Tzeng, Trevor Darrell, and Kate Saenko. 2017. "Simultaneous deep transfer across domains and tasks." In *Domain Adaptation in Computer Vision Applications*, 173–187. New York: Springer.

Hogg, Michael A., and Scott A. Reid. 2006. "Social Identity, Self Categorization, and the Communication of Group Norms." *Communication Theory* 16: 7–30. https://doi.org/10.1111/j.1468-2885.2006.00003.x

Holton, Gerald. 1978. *The Scientific Imagination: Case Studies.* Cambridge: Cambridge University Press.

Horn, Stacy. 1998. *Cyberville: Clicks, Culture, and the Creation of an Online Town.* New York: Warner Books.

Hutchins, Edwin. 1995a. *Cognition in the Wild.* Cambridge, MA: MIT Press.

Hutchins, Edwin. 1995b. "How a Cockpit Remembers Its Speed." *Cognitive Science* 19: 265–288. https://doi.org/10.1207/s15516709cog1903_1

Ingold, John. 2018. "We went to a flat-earth convention and found a lesson about the future of post-truth life." The Colorado Sun. https://coloradosun.com/2018/11/20/flat-earth-convention-denver-post-truth

Jensen, Carlos, and Colin Potts. 2004. "Privacy policies as decision-making tools: an evaluation of online privacy notices." *Proceedings of the Conference on Human Factors in Computing Systems (CHI).* https://doi.org/10.1145/985692 .985752

Jhaver, Shagun, Iris Birman, Eric Gilbert, and Amy Bruckman. 2019. "Human–Machine Collaboration for Content Regulation: The Case of Reddit Automoderator." *ACM Transactions on Computer-Human Interaction* 26 (5). https://doi.org/10.1145/3338243

Kant, E., and H. J. Patton. 1964. *Groundwork for the Metaphysic of Morals.* New York: Harper & Row.

Khalifa, Nour Eldeen, Mohamed Hamed Taha, Aboul Ella Hassanien, and Ibrahim Selim. 2018. "Deep Galaxy V2: Robust Deep Convolutional Neural Networks for Galaxy Morphology Classifications." *Proceedings of the 2018 International Conference on Computing Sciences and Engineering, ICCSE 2018.* https://doi.org/10.1109/ICCSE1.2018.8374210

Khatib, Firas, Frank Dimaio, Seth Cooper, et al. 2010. "Crystal structure of a monomeric retroviral protease solved by protein folding game players." *Nature Structural and Molecular Biology* 18 (10): 1175–1177. https://doi.org/10.1038/nsmb.2119

Kietzmann, Jan, Linda W. Lee, Ian P. McCarthy, and Tim C. Kietzmann. 2019. "Deepfakes: Trick or treat?" *Business Horizons* 63 (2): 135–146. https://doi.org/10.1016/j.bushor.2019.11.006

Kim, Amy Jo. 2000. *Community Building on the Web.* Berkeley, CA: Peachpit Press.

King, Daniel, Paul Delfabbro, Sally Gainsbury, et al. 2019. "Unfair play? Video games as exploitative monetized services: an examination of game patents from a consumer protection perspective." *Computers in Human Behavior* 101: 131–143. https://doi.org/10.1016/j.chb.2019.07.017

Kirchner, Lauren. 2011. "AOL Settled with Unpaid 'Volunteers' for $15 Million." *Columbia Journalism Review.* https://archives.cjr .org/the_news_frontier/aol_settled_with_unpaid_volunt.php

Kovach, Steve. 2019. "Alphabet had more than $70 billion in market cap wiped out, and it says YouTube is one of the problems." CNBC. www.cnbc.com/2019/04/30/youtube-algorithm-changes-negatively-impact-google-ad-revenue.html

Lakoff, George. 1987. *Women, Fire, and Dangerous Things: What Categories Reveal about the Mind*. Chicago, IL: University of Chicago Press.

Landrum, Ashley R., Alex Olshanksy, and Othello Richards. 2019. Differential susceptibility to misleading flat earth arguments on YouTube. *Media Psychology* 24 (1): 136–165. https://doi.org/10.1080/15213269.2019.1669461

Lapinski, Maria Knight, and Rajiv N. Rimal. 2005. "An Explication of Social Norms." *Communications Theory* 15 (2): 127–147. https://doi.org/10.1111/j.1468-2885.2005.tb00329.x

Larsson, K. Sune. 1995. "The dissemination of false data through inadequate citation." *Journal of Internal Medicine* 238 (5): 445–450. https://doi.org/10.1111/j.1365-2796.1995.tb01222.x

Latour, Bruno, Steve Woolgar, and Jonas Salk. 1986. *Laboratory Life*. Princeton, NJ: Princeton University Press.

Lave, Jean, and Etienne Wenger. 1991. *Situated Learning: Legitimate Peripheral Participation*. Cambridge: Cambridge University Press.

Leavitt, Alex. 2015. "'This Is a Throwaway Account'." *Proceedings of the 18th ACM Conference on Computer Supported Cooperative Work & Social Computing (CSCW)*. https://doi.org/10.1145/2675133.2675175

LeBaron, Geoff. 2019. "The 119th Christmas Bird Count summary." www.audubon.org/news/the-119th christmas-bird-count-summary

Lessig, Lawrence. 1999. *CODE and Other Laws of Cyberspace*. New York: Basic Books.

Leuf, Bo, and Ward Cunningham. 2001. *The Wiki Way: Collaboration and Sharing on the Internet*. Boston, MA: Addison Wesley.

Levin, S. 2018. "Uber drivers often make below minimum wage, report finds." *Guardian*, March 5. www.theguardian.com/technology/2018/mar/01/uber-lyft-driver-wages-median-report

Luther, Kurt, and Amy Bruckman. 2011. "Leadership and Success Factors in Online Creative Collaboration." *IEEE Potentials* 30 (5). https://doi.org/10.1109/MPOT.2011.941499

Luther, Kurt, Kelly Caine, Kevin Ziegler, and Amy Bruckman. 2010. "Why it works (when it works): success factors in online creative collaboration." *GROUP '10: Proceedings of the 16th ACM International Conference on Supporting Group Work (GROUP).* https://doi.org/10.1145/1880071.1880073

Luther, Kurt, Casey Fiesler, and Amy Bruckman. 2013. "Redistributing leadership in online creative collaboration." *Proceedings of the 2013 Conference on Computer Supported Cooperative Work (CSCW).* https://doi.org/10.1145/2441776.2441891

Manjoo, Farhad. 2019. "How Black People Use Twitter." *Slate.* https://slate.com/technology/2010/08/how-black-people-use-twitter.html

Mastodon. 2019. "Statement on Gab's fork of Mastodon." Mastodon blog, July 4. https://blog.joinmastodon.org/2019/07/statement-on-gabs-fork-of-mastodon

Matias, J. Nathan. 2019. "Preventing harassment and increasing group participation through social norms in 2,190 online science discussions." *Proceedings of the National Academy of Sciences* 116 (20): 201813486. https://doi.org/10.1073/pnas.1813486116

Matias, J. Nathan, and Merry Mou. 2018. "CivilServant: Community-Led Experiments in Platform Governance." *Proceedings of the Conference on Human Factors in Computing Systems.* https://doi.org/10.1145/3173574.3173583

McDonald, Aleecia, and Lorrie Cranor. 2008. "The Cost of Reading Privacy Policies." *I/S* 4 (3). https://heinonline.org/HOL/P?h=hein.journals/isjlpsoc4&i=563

Mesgari, Mostafa, Chitu Okoli, Mohamad Mehdi, Finn Arup Nielsen, and Arto Lanamaki. 2015. "'The sum of all human knowledge': A systematic review of scholarly research on the content of Wikipedia." *Journal for the Association for Information Science and Technology* 66 (2): 219–245. https://doi .org/https://doi.org/10.1002/asi.23172

Mihalascu, Dan. 2020. "Whispers Is an Exclusive Social Network for Owners of New Rolls-Royce Cars." *Carscoops*. www .carscoops.com/2020/02/whispers-is-an-exclusive-social-network-for-owners-of-new-rolls-royce-cars

Millikan, Robert Andrews. 1909. "A new modification of the cloud method of measuring the elementary electrical charge, and the most probable value of that charge." *Physical Review* 29 (6): 560–561. https://resolver.caltech.edu/CaltechAUTHORS:MIL.pro9

Mockus, Audris, R. T. Fielding, and J. D. Herbsleb. 2002. "Two case studies of open source software development: Apache and Mozilla." *ACM Transactions on Software Engineering and Methodology (TOSEM)* 11 (3): 309–346. https://doi.org/10.1145/ 567793.567795

Mozilla. n.d. "We're building a better Internet." www.mozilla.org/ en-US/mission

Nakakoji, Kumiyo, Yasuhiro Yamamoto, Yoshiyuki Nishinaka, Kouichi Kishida, and Yunwen Ye. 2002. "Evolution patterns of open-source software systems and communities." *Proceedings of the International Workshop on Principles of Software Evolution – IWPSE '02*. https://doi.org/10.1145/512035 .512055

Nickerson, Raymond S. 1998. "Confirmation Bias: A Ubiquitous Phenomenon in Many Guises." *Review of General Psychology* 2 (2): 175–220. https://doi.org/10.1037/1089-2680.2.2.175

Nonnecke, Blair, and Jenny Preece. 2000. "Lurker demographics: counting the silent." *Proceedings of the SIGCHI Conference on Human Factors in Computing Systems (CHI)*. https://doi.org/10 .1145/332040.332409

Nyhan, Brendan, and Jason Reifler. 2016. "When Corrections Fail: The Persistence of Political Misperceptions." *Political Behavior* 32 (2): 303–330. www.jstor.org/stable/40587320

Oldenburg, Ray. 1989. *The Great Good Place*. New York: Paragon House.

Oxford Dictionaries. 2016. "Word of the year." https://en .oxforddictionaries.com/word-of-the-year/word-of-the-year-2016

Parrish, Julia K., Hillary Burgess, Jake F. Weltzin, et al. 2018. "Exposing the Science in Citizen Science: Fitness to Purpose and Intentional Design." *Integrative and Comparative Biology* 58(1): 150–160. http://dx.doi.org/10.1093/icb/icy032

Pater, Jessica A., Yacin Nadji, Elizabeth D. Mynatt, and Amy Bruckman. 2014. "Just awful enough: the functional dysfunction of the Something Awful forums." *CHI '14: Proceedings of the SIGCHI Conference on Human Factors in Computing Systems*. https://doi.org/10.1145/2556288.2557193

PatientsLikeMe. 2018. "Bibliography of PatientsLikeMe." www .patientslikeme.com/research/publications

Pettegree, Andrew. 2014. *The Invention of News*. New Haven, CT: Yale University Press.

Phillips, Whitney. 2015. *This Is Why We Can't Have Nice Things, Mapping the Relationship between Trolling and Mainstream Culture*. Cambridge, MA: MIT Press.

Pinkowski, Jennifer. 2010. "How to Classify a Million Galaxies in Three Weeks." *Time*. http://content.time.com/time/health/ article/0,8599,1975296,00.html

Postigo, Hector. 2003. "Emerging Sources of Labor on the Internet: The Case of America Online Volunteers." *International Review of Social History* 48 (Suppl. 11): 205–223. https://doi.org/10.1017/ S0020859003001329

Putnam, Robert. 1995. "Bowling Alone: America's Declining Social Capital." *Journal of Democracy* 6 (1). https://link.springer.com/ chapter/10.1007/978-1-349-62965-7_12

Quinn, Michael J. 2017. *Ethics for the Information Age*. 7th ed. Harlow: Pearson.

Quittner, Josh. 1994. "The War Between alt.tasteless and rec.pets. cats." *Wired*. www.wired.com/1994/05/alt-tasteless

Radiolab. 2018. Post no evil (podcast). WNYC.

Raymond, Eric. 1999. "The cathedral and the bazaar." *Knowledge, Technology, & Policy* 12 (3): 23–49. https://link.springer.com/article/10.1007/s12130-999-1026-0

Rekdal, Ole Bjorn. 2014. "Academic urban legends." *Social Studies of Science* 44 (4): 638–654. https://doi.org/10.1177%2F0306312714535679

Resnick, Paul. 2001. "Beyond bowling together: sociotechnical capital." In John M. Carroll (ed.), *HCI in the New Millenium*, 247–272. Boston, MA: Addison Wesley.

Rheingold, Howard. 1993. *The Virtual Community: Homesteading on the Electronic Frontier*. Reading, MA: Addison Wesley. https://www.rheingold.com/vc/book/intro.html

Roberts, Sarah T. 2017. "Social Media's Silent Filter." *The Atlantic*. www.theatlantic.com/technology/archive/2017/03/commercial-content-moderation/518796

Ronson, Jon. 2015. "How one stupid tweet blew up Justine Sacco's life." *New York Times Magazine*, February 15. www.nytimes.com/2015/02/15/magazine/how-one-stupid-tweet-ruined-justine-saccos-life.html

Rood, Vanessa, and Amy Bruckman. 2009. "Member behavior in company online communities." *GROUP '09: Proceedings of the ACM 2009 International Conference on Supporting Group Work (GROUP)*. https://doi.org/10.1145/1531674.1531705

Rosch, Eleanor. 1999. "Principles of categorization." In Eric Margolis and Stephen Laurence (eds.), *Concepts: Core Readings*, 189–206. Cambridge, MA: MIT Press.

Rosenblatt, Kalhan. 2019. "YouTube announces it will no longer recommend conspiracy videos." NBC News, February 10.

www.nbcnews.com/tech/tech-news/youtube-announces-it-will-no-longer-recommend-conspiracy-videos-n969856

Rosenzweig, Roy. 2006. "Can History Be Open Source? Wikipedia and the Future of the Past." *Journal of American History* 93 (1): 117–146. https://doi.org/10.2307/4486062

Roth, Yoel, and Ashita Achuthan. 2020. "Building rules in public: Our approach to synthetic & manipulated media." Twitter blog. https://blog.twitter.com/en_us/topics/company/2020/new-approach-to-synthetic-and-manipulated-media.html

Roth, Yoel, and Nick Pickles. 2020. "Updating our approach to misleading information." Twitter blog. https://blog.twitter.com/en_us/topics/product/2020/updating-our-approach-to-misleading-information.html

Rotman, Dana, Jen Hammock, Jenny Preece, Derek Hansen, and Carol Boston. 2014. "Motivations Affecting Initial and Long-Term Participation in Citizen Science Projects in Three Countries." *iConference 2014 Proceedings*. https://doi.org/10.9776/14054

Saenko, Kate, Brian Kulis, Mario Fritz, and Trevor Darrell. 2010. "Adapting Visual Category Models to New Domains." *European Conference on Computer Vision*. https://link.springer.com/chapter/10.1007/978-3-642-15561-1_16

Sample, Ian. 2019. "Study blames YouTube for rise in number of Flat Earthers." *Guardian*. www.theguardian.com/science/2019/feb/17/study-blames-youtube-for-rise-in-number-of-flat-earthers

Sandefur, Rebecca, and Edward Laumann. 1998. "A paradigm for social capital." *Rationality and Society* 10 (4): 481–501. https://doi.org/10.1177%2F104346398010004005

Sandvig, Christian. 2012. "Connection at Ewiiaapaayp Mountain." In L. Nakamura and P. Chow-White (eds.), *Race after the Internet*, 168–200. New York: Routledge.

Sanger, Larry. 2005. "The early history of NuPedia and Wikipedia: a memoir." In C. DiBona, M. Stone, and D. Cooper (eds.), *Open Source 2.0*, chapter 20. Sebastopol, CA: O'Reilly Press.

Sauermann, Henry, and Chiara Franzoni. 2015. "Crowd science user contribution patterns and their implications." *Proceedings of the National Academy of Sciences* 112 (3): 679–684. https://doi.org/10.1073/pnas.1408907112

Schank, Roger, and Robert P. Abelson. 2013. *Scripts, Plans, Goals and Understanding: An Inquiry into Human Knowledge.* Hove: Psychology Press.

Schwartz, Oscar. 2018. "You thought fake news was bad? Deep fakes are where truth goes to die." *Guardian.* www.theguardian.com/technology/2018/nov/12/deep-fakes-fake-news-truth

Shachaf, Pnina, and Noriko Hara. 2010. "Beyond vandalism: Wikipedia trolls." *Journal of Information Science* 36 (5): 357–370. http://eprints.rclis.org/15530/1/wikipediatrolls.pdf

Shahani, Aarti. 2016. "With 'Napalm Girl,' Facebook Humans (Not Algorithms) Struggle to Be Editor." All Tech Considered, National Public Radio. www.npr.org/sections/alltechconsidered/2016/09/10/493454256/with-napalm-girl-facebook-humans-not-algorithms-struggle-to-be-editor

Shuler, Doug. 1994. "Community networks: building a new participatory medium." *Communications of the ACM* 37 (1): 38–51. https://doi.org/10.1145/175222.175225

Silvertown, Jonathan. 2009. "A new dawn for citizen science." *Trends in Ecology & Evolution* 24 (9): 467–471. https://doi.org/10.1016/j.tree.2009.03.017

Spotts, Peter N. 2007. "Identifying galaxies: everyman's task – CSMonitor.com." *Christian Science Monitor.* www.csmonitor.com/2007/0716/p03s01-ussc.html

Stanford Encyclopedia of Philosophy. 2016. "Virtue Ethics." *Stanford Encyclopedia of Philosophy.* https://plato.stanford.edu/entries/ethics-virtue

Starbird, Kate, Ahmer Arif, and Tom Wilson. 2019. "Disinformation as Collaborative Work: Surfacing the Participatory Nature of

Strategic Information Operation." *PACM on Human–Computer Interaction 3 (CSCW).* https://doi.org/10.1145/3359229

Stephenson, Neal. 2019. *Fall; or, Dodge in Hell.* New York: William Morrow.

Steup, Matthias. 2016. "Epistemology." *Stanford Encyclopedia of Philosophy.* https://plato.stanford.edu/archives/fall2016/entries/epistemology/

Stewart, Emily. 2018. "Lawmakers seem confused about what Facebook does – and how to fix it." *Vox.* www.vox.com/policy-and-politics/2018/4/10/17222062/mark-zuckerberg-testimony-graham-facebook-regulations

Sunstein, Cass R. 2018. *#Republic: Divided Democracy in the Age of Social Media.* Princeton, NJ: Princeton University Press.

Swanson, Alexandra, Margaret Kosmala, Chris Lintott, and Craig Packer. 2016. "A generalized approach for producing, quantifying, and validating citizen science data from wildlife images." *Conservation Biology* 30 (3): 520–531. https://doi.org/10.1111/cobi.12695

Toma, Catalina L., Jeffrey T. Hancock, and Nicole B. Ellison. 2008. "Separating Fact from Fiction: An Examination of Deceptive Self-Presentation in Online Dating Profiles." *Personality and Social Psychology Bulletin* 34 (8): 1023–1036. https://doi.org/10.1177/0146167208318067

Tufekci, Zeynep. 2018. "YouTube, the Great Radicalizer." *New York Times,* March 10. www.nytimes.com/2018/03/10/opinion/sunday/youtube-politics-radical.html

Turkle, Sherry. 1984. *The Second Self: Computers and the Human Spirit.* New York: Simon & Schuster.

Turkle, Sherry. 1995. *Life on the Screen: Identity in the Age of the Internet.* New York: Simon & Schuster.

United Nations. n.d. "United Nations Strategy and Plan of Action on Hate Speech." www.un.org/en/genocideprevention/hate-speech-strategy.shtml

Van Gelder, Lindsy. 1985. "The strange case of the electronic lover." *Ms. Magazine.* http://lindsyvangelder.com/clips/strange-case-electronic-lover

Viegas, Fernanda, Martin Watternberg, and Kushal David. 2004. "Studying cooperation and conflict between users with history flow visualizations." *Proceedings of the SIGCHI Conference on Human Factors in Computing Systems (CHI).* https://doi.org/10.1145/985692.985765

Vitak, Jessica. 2012. "The Impact of Context Collapse and Privacy on Social Network Site Disclosures." *Journal of Broadcasting and Electronic Media* 56 (4): 451–470. https://doi.org/10.1080/08838151.2012.732140

Von Ahn, Luis. 2006. "Games with a purpose." *Computer* 39 (6): 92–94. https://doi.org/10.1109/MC.2006.196

Von Ahn, Luis, and Laura Dabbish. 2004. "Labeling images with a computer game." *Proceedings of the 2004 Conference on Human Factors in Computing Systems.* https://doi.org/10.1145/985692.985733

Welch, Brady. 2017. "People from around the globe met for the first Flat Earth Conference." *Vice.* https://news.vice.com/en_us/article/ywnnaj/people-from-around-the-globe-met-for-the-first-flat-earth-conference

Welch, C. 2018. "Facebook will give all US users helpful context about articles shared in News Feed." *The Verge.* www.theverge.com/2018/4/3/17193750/facebook-news-feed-articles-publisher

Wellman, B., A. Q. Haase, J. Witte, and K. Hampton. 2001. "Does the Internet increase, decrease, or supplement social capital?" *American Behavioral Scientist* 45 (3): 436. https://doi.org/10.1177/00027640121957286

Whyte, William. 1964. "How to Live in a City." www.youtube.com/watch?v=2Je6Dko6mm4

Wiggins, A., and K. Crowston. 2011. "From Conservation to Crowd Sourcing: A Typology of Citizen Science." *44th Hawaii International Conference on System Sciences.* https://doi.org/10 .1109/HICSS.2011.207

Wong, Carrie Julia, and Sam Levine. 2020. "Twitter labels Trump's false claims with warning for first time." *Guardian*, May 26. www.theguardian.com/us-news/2020/may/26/trump-twitter-fact-check-warning-label

York, Jillian C. 2012. "2012 in Review: How Blasphemy Laws Are Stifling Free Expression Worldwide." www.eff.org/deeplinks/ 2012/12/2012-review-how-blasphemy-laws-are-stifling-free-expression-worldwide

York, Jillian C., Corynne McSherry, and Danny O'Brien. 2021. "Beyond Platforms: Private Censorship, Parler, and the Stack." Electronic Frontier Foundation. www.eff.org/deeplinks/2021/ 01/beyond-platforms-private-censorship-parler-and-stack

Zetlin, Minda. 2018. "The 9 Weirdest and Most Hilarious Questions Congress Asked Mark Zuckerberg." *Inc.* www.inc .com/minda-zetlin/mark-zuckerberg-congress-hearings-funny-stupid-questions.html

Zuboff, Shoshana. 2019. *The Age of Surveillance Capitalism.* New York: PublicAffairs.

Zuboff, Shoshana 2020. "Opinion: You Are Now Remotely Controlled." *New York Times*, January 24. www.nytimes.com/ 2020/01/24/opinion/sunday/surveillance-capitalism.html

# INDEX